#DUPED

How the Anti-gun Lobby Exploits
the Parkland School Shooting—and
How Gun Owners Can Fight Back

10639472

New York Times Bestselling Author
MARK W. SMITH

A BOMBARDIER BOOKS BOOK
An Imprint of Post Hill Press
ISBN: 978-1-64293-011-5
ISBN (eBook): 978-1-64293-012-2

#Duped:
How the Anti-gun Lobby Exploits the Parkland School
Shooting—and How Gun Owners Can Fight Back

Cover Design by Cody Corcoran

Post Hill Press
New York • Nashville
posthillpress.com

Published in the United States of America

TABLE OF CONTENTS

Introduction: The Kids' Table...........5

Part 1: From the Mouths of Babes? Hardly. 13

Chapter 1: From Trojan Horses to Trojan Ponies...........15

Chapter 2: Do As I Say, Not As I Do (Because I'm More Important Than You)...........29

Part 2: Your Intellectual Ammunition: Exposing the Gun Grabbers' Favorite Myths...........39

Chapter 3: *Gun Grabber Myth #1*
"Nobody Needs a Gun"...........41

Chapter 4: *Gun Grabber Myth #2*
"You Don't Need a Gun. Highly Trained Government Professionals Are Here to Protect You."...........57

Chapter 5: *Gun Grabber Myth #3*
"Guns Are the Problem" But Somehow Other Instruments of Violence Are Not...........73

Chapter 6: *Gun Grabber Myth #4*
"We Need to Ban Assault Weapons"...........89

Chapter 7: *Gun Grabber Myth #5*
"Gun-Free Zones Are Nirvana"...........101

Chapter 8: *Gun Grabber Myth #6*
"It's Too Easy to Buy a Gun"...........115

Chapter 9: *Gun Grabber Myth #7*
"The Second Amendment Doesn't Apply to Modern America"...........127

Conclusion: What's Your Plan?...143

Endnotes...151

About the Author..196

Introduction
The Kids' Table

On April 24, 2018, *TIME* magazine held a glittering gala in Manhattan honoring the one hundred most influential people of the year. Among the honorees were five high school students from Parkland, Florida—survivors of the horrific mass shooting at Marjory Stoneman Douglas High School two months earlier.

These five young people—David Hogg, Emma Gonzalez, Jaclyn Corin, Cameron Kasky, and Alex Wind—have emerged as the faces of the #NeverAgain anti-gun movement. None other than former president Barack Obama profiled the Parkland students for *TIME*. Obama gushed about the "young leaders," saying they "don't intimidate easily" and are "comfortable speaking truth to power."[1] At the gala, the Parkland kids were "the real stars of the night," according to the *New York Post*. Celebrities and fellow honorees "swarmed the students."[2]

But the *Post* story highlighted an unusual aspect of how the Parkland students were treated: "they'd been relegated to what amounted to the kids' table," stuck way up "at the back of the top tier of Jazz at Lincoln Center," where the party was held.[3]

This is the perfect metaphor for understanding the Parkland kids and their relationship to the "new" gun control movement.

Think about it: Ever since the Parkland shootings, David Hogg and his anti-gun classmates have been the toast of the media, interviewed everywhere from CBS to CNN to NPR to MSNBC to HBO. David Hogg and his sister even received a major book deal from Random House. Politicians, pundits, celebrities, and activists have hailed these kids for their courage, wisdom, and leadership.

But really, those politicians, pundits, celebrities, and activists are using the "young leaders" to advance their own longstanding agenda: gun control.

They're happy to send David Hogg out on every network, celebrate his "courage" for speaking out, and portray him as the "leader" of a new movement. But behind the scenes, the Parkland kids *aren't* leaders. They're stuck at the kids' table while the activists and moneymen orchestrate this "new" gun control movement.

In reality, it's just a repackaging of the same old anti-gun coalition. The messenger is new, but the message is old.

This isn't the first time the gun controllers rushed to exploit tragedy. Take a look at this email exchange between former Obama chief of staff, now Chicago mayor Rahm Emanuel, and Obama's Education Secretary Arne Duncan, *just two days after the 2012 Sandy*

Hook killings and before the funerals could even be held. In an email exchange titled "CT shootings," Duncan and Emanuel strategized:

> Duncan: *"What are your thoughts?"*
> Emanuel: *"Go for a vote this week before it fades. Tap peoples [sic] emotion. Make it simple assault weapons."*
> Duncan: *"Yup- thanks."*
> Emanuel: *"When I did brady bill and assault weapons for clinton we always made it simple. Criminals or war weapons."*
> Duncan: *"Gun show loophole? Database? Cop-killer bullets? Too complicated?"*
> Emanuel: *"Cop killer maybe. The other no."*[4]

Emanuel served as the Obama White House Chief of Staff from January 2009 to October 2010. He famously said, "You never want a serious crisis to go to waste. And what I mean by that is an opportunity to do things that you think you could not do before."[5]

On the coattails of one of the most horrific school shootings in our nation's history, the gun grabbers' first priority was developing their national strategy to take away your guns.

Sound familiar?

Let's Have *That* Debate

Let's set aside all the effusive praise for those Parkland students who support gun control and who have been adopted by America's gun control lobby. Instead, let's take a look at what the #NeverAgain kids actually say.

When you examine their arguments closely—as I will in this book—you'll see that they don't even really *offer* arguments. They do little more than string together appeals to emotion, ad hominem attacks, and warmed-over gun-control rhetoric.

So, why are America's anti-gunners so excited about having the Parkland students join their so-called movement? Why does the mainstream media devote countless hours to airing interviews of these students who in turn attack guns and gun owners? Because the gun grabbers' previous efforts at radical gun control have mostly failed.

The gun control movement has been around for decades and has largely been in retreat over the last few decades. Today, the country has record numbers of firearms, gun owners, and individuals allowed to conceal carry handguns.

The U.S. Supreme Court has found that the Second Amendment protects the individual right to bear arms. President Donald Trump made a point to speak at each of the last several NRA annual conventions. And President Trump defeated an overtly anti-gun politician in Hillary Rodham Clinton in the last presidential election.

In football, when your team is far behind on the scoreboard, you throw a desperation "Hail Mary" pass to try to save the day. The gun grabbers recognize that they need to do the same. This is why the anti-gun movement, including their urban handmaidens in the mainstream media, have so heartily embraced the Parkland students. It also explains that while the media saturates the airwaves and cable networks with David Hogg and his anti-gun peers, that same media largely ignores the Parkland students (and others) who support gun rights—such as student Kyle Kashuv.

The gun control movement relies on stale, old, and tired arguments that have largely been factually debunked and mostly rejected by Americans. Because the gun controllers do not have the facts, history, or logic on their side, they must rely heavily on appeals to emotion and on other flawed arguments. This is why the old-line gun control movement has become so enamored with the anti-gun Parkland students, because they, too, advance their arguments using appeals mostly to emotion and personal attacks.

Make no mistake, the #NeverAgain kids have the right to express themselves. That they experienced such a traumatic event makes it easy to understand why they want to participate in debates about school and public safety.

I, personally, welcome the opportunity to help those same students understand the importance and value of firearms. The students have the right to speak out, and also the right to be wrong (or right) about gun control. But they do not have the right to ignore the facts, the evidence, or the logic in favor of guns, especially when doing so comes at the expense of long-standing and life-saving Constitutional freedoms and rights.

As they get older and have more responsibilities put upon them, the #NeverAgain kids may start to feel differently about gun control. Some will start families, others may find themselves living alone in high crime areas or employed in occupations that put them at a greater risk of becoming a victim. All will be forced to make informed decisions about how best to protect themselves and their families from bad people who want to hurt them.

So, let's set emotion aside and discuss the facts. Let's have *that* debate.

In this spirit, *#Duped* will do two things:

- strip bare how young people like the Parkland students are exploited for political gain and to short-circuit any legitimate debate, and
- lay out the truth about guns and safety that you won't hear in emotion-drenched media coverage.

What's at Stake: Your Freedom and Your Life

David Hogg and his fellow Parkland students have become the faces of a gun control movement that seeks to deprive law-abiding Americans of our right to bear arms and our ability to protect ourselves, our families, and our communities from criminals and crazies.

That's why all this matters. That's what's at stake: your safety and the safety of your loved ones.

What's at stake, too, are your freedoms. The #NeverAgain movement likes to position itself as an heir to the civil rights movement. That's why you've seen so many signs at anti-gun rallies that say things like, "Our lives are worth more than your guns," "My right to safety > your right to a rifle," and "I hope to have as many rights as a gun someday."

But the gun control movement is *not* about civil rights. Previous civil rights movements in U.S. history sought to *expand* individual freedoms. Hogg and his peers—backed by hypocritical celebrities, billionaires, and politicians—want to *shrink your* freedoms by depriving you of your fundamental right to self-defense.

You need to understand this. And you need to understand all the myths about guns and safety that are going unchallenged in the current climate, where emotion often wins out over facts and logic.

The facts matter because here's the truth: *What you don't know about guns can kill you.*

If the gun grabbers win the day with their misleading arguments, you and your family will be much less safe. Make no mistake, the ultimate goal of the anti-gun movement is complete civilian disarmament.

In this book, you'll learn the truth about the #NeverAgain movement and get the facts you need to counter the gun grabbers' favorite (and false!) talking points.

Part 1

From the Mouths of Babes? Hardly.

Meet the new gun control movement, same as the old gun control movement.

Ever since the Parkland school shootings, the #NeverAgain kids have become the face of gun control. But are these students really "leaders" speaking "truth to power," as we hear all the time?

No, they're sympathetic victims who are effective at advancing the same, warmed-over ideas on gun control.

Here you'll learn the truth about the "new" gun control movement.

The hypocrisy is shocking: the celebrities, politicians, and billionaires who are leading the campaign to ban guns surround themselves with armed guards. And they're duping the Parkland kids into renouncing rights that they have never had—or even been old enough to exercise.

Chapter 1
From Trojan Horses
to Trojan Ponies

When the artificial grass known as AstroTurf was first installed in the Houston Astrodome in 1966, little did its creators know that the venerable name of this space-age product would come to define fake politics.

Political operatives and community organizers prize "grassroots" movements because they suggest an organic groundswell of support for a cause. Then there's AstroTurf, a term used to describe a phony grassroots effort designed to appear organic when, in fact, it's a highly orchestrated campaign largely bankrolled by a few wealthy supporters.

That is precisely what we are seeing with the latest iteration of the gun control movement. The young people hailed as the movement's leaders are being heralded specifically for the purpose of putting an unimpeachable face on the effort to erode the constitutional rights of law-abiding citizens.

Take, for example, the so-called national student walkout in March 2018. The media were diligently promoting the misbehavior of students in cities large and small, suggesting that this was a bunch of kids demanding change. Less obvious from the media coverage was the fact that the entire effort to cut class was orchestrated by something called the Women's March.[6]

The Women's March, you may recall, organized nationwide gatherings of leftists following the inauguration of Donald Trump in January 2017, most notably on the National Mall in Washington, D.C. Billed as a demonstration of female empowerment, the event quickly devolved into an array of unhinged rants sprinkled with all manner of weirdness and vulgarity.[7]

One of the highlights of the D.C. event came when pop singer Madonna took to the stage to say she had "thought an awful lot about blowing up the White House."[8]

Although no one believes that the aging songstress would actually blow up the White House, the line illustrated that the Women's March is less about women and more about promoting your garden-variety left-wing agenda—including gun control.

Fast-forward thirteen months. The Women's March helped orchestrate the national school walkout to promote gun control. This call to action sent a signal flare to progressive liberals across the country, particularly teachers and school administrators, to encourage students to violate school policies against skipping class so they could be used to agitate for gun control.[9] It was a brilliant form of manipulation, because cutting class is a very attractive proposition for an adolescent who is dealing with his or her inner rebel (and seeking to skip Geometry class).

With the explicit or tacit approval of some teachers and school administrators, thousands of students did indeed cut class for a while on March 14, 2018.[10] And as the media engaged in wall-to-wall news coverage of the walkouts, we were led to believe that these were just a bunch of concerned kids who, of their own volition, gathered to raise their voices to end school violence.

AstroTurf.

A national group of progressive liberals orchestrated the walkouts to position as many children as possible to be the new face of gun control. And a lot of kids, understandably, took part. After all, they're kids, and grown-ups were offering them a free pass to break the rules.

Not reported was how many students chose *not* to cut class that day.[11] Both the Associated Press and *The Washington Post* reported that across the entire country, only some "tens of thousands" of students participated in the high school walkout.[12] The order of magnitude of the "tens of thousands" was left ambiguous. Even if 90,000 students walked out (highly doubtful), that would mean that *less than 1 percent* of the 16 million American high school students[13] demonstrated their support for the anti-freedom, anti-Constitutional, gun control agenda by skipping class.

The media almost entirely ignored the young people who chose *not* to be exploited. So in most cases we have no idea how many students decided against walking out of class. But anecdotal information suggests they may represent a sizable group, maybe even a silent majority.

For example, at Brattleboro Union High School, in my home state of Vermont, approximately 650 students—at least 70 percent of the student body—chose *not* to protest. But you would never know this from the reporting of the local press. The *Brattleboro Reformer* ran two front-page stories and four front-page photos with the breathless headline "Brattleboro Union High School students demand change."[14]

How many non-protesting students did the *Reformer* quote for its stories? Zero.

AstroTurf.

Then there's the March for Our Lives, a series of demonstrations across the nation on March 24 exploiting kids and willing adults to agitate for gun control. Exploitation doesn't come cheap. It requires a lot of money to pay for everything involved in manipulating kids in hundreds of cities and towns. Anyone who saw news coverage of the D.C. march saw the enormous stage, the Jumbotrons, the towers of public address speakers, and all the trappings of a well-organized, well-executed, well-funded and professional political event.

You are naïve if you think a bunch of seventeen-year-old kids, who can't rent cars, get hotel rooms, or legally enter into binding contracts, organized this major, multimillion-dollar event on their own. Such a sophisticated technological and logistical effort had to be orchestrated by folks with experience in the art and business of large-scale public promotions and events. No amount of drama club training, babysitting or bake sale experience could enable a group of seventeen-year-olds to pull this off.

So, who bought all this? A synopsis provided by the Capital Research Center reveals a list of the usual suspects who tend to bankroll left-wing activities: "Steven Spielberg, Jeffrey Katzenberg, George Clooney, Oprah Winfrey, and the fashion company Gucci reportedly donated $500,000 each to the group. Salesforce CEO Marc Benioff pledged another $1 million."[15] Coincidentally, each of these folks supported Hilary Rodham Clinton for president.[16]

AstroTurf. It's all AstroTurf.

Exploiting Emotions

Aristotle taught us that appeals to emotion are logical fallacies. He wrote: "The arousing of prejudice, pity, anger, and similar emotions has nothing to do with the essential facts but is merely a personal appeal to the man who is judging the case."[17] There's a reason trial juries are instructed by the presiding judge not to allow their emotions to dictate their decisions.

But appeals to emotion are pretty much all that the new gun controllers advance. They do it by rolling out sympathetic spokespeople: survivors of horrifying mass shootings, and children to boot. And therefore David Hogg, Emma Gonzalez, and other survivors of the Parkland school shootings have become the new faces of the movement. Not surprisingly, neither the pro-gun students nor those students suing the Broward County police officers for malfeasance were selected for stardom by the legacy media.[18]

Behind the scenes are left-wing activist groups orchestrating the protests and celebrities bankrolling their efforts. And out front you have the innocent young victims, who receive fawning media coverage and praise from the usual anti-gun politicians.

The organizers of these AstroTurf campaigns are playing on emotion to prevent any real discussion of the serious issues at hand. They know that they can dismiss anyone who dares question the claims these young people make. All they must do is charge their critics with "attacking the victims." With that, the discussion is cut off. The debate ends. Done.

But here's the thing: at seventeen or eighteen very few of us have original thoughts on politics and policy.

Most teenagers have their teachers' thoughts, their parents' thoughts, their peers' thoughts, and social media's thoughts.

Few people would look to a seventeen-year-old for any original thinking.

And yet here's Barack Obama proclaiming of these marching minions: "Our children are calling us to account.... They have the power so often inherent in youth: to see the world anew; to reject the old constraints, outdated conventions and cowardice too often dressed up as wisdom."[19]

If we are to "see the world anew" and "reject old constraints and outdated conventions," we, the benighted adults of America, will soon be the beneficiaries of this new wisdom—the "wisdom" of high school students rehashing long-rejected gun control arguments.

What high school student could resist such absurd flattery?

That it took thousands of years of trial and error for Western civilization to come up with a reasonably humane system for all of us to live together peaceably with a fair amount of personal freedom doesn't seem to trouble our former president. He's ready to move on to the broad sunlit uplands of our bright new future led by these children.

Of course, the adults spending millions to support the student protesters encourage this nonsense to advance their real agenda: gun control (and, ultimately, gun confiscation).

Their slogan might be *Make America Australia Again*—or maybe *Make America England Again*, or even *Make America Venezuela Again*.

We can reasonably assume that none of those millions of dollars will be going to subsidize the efforts of those students who don't walk out and don't agree with David Hogg and Emma Gonzalez.

One should think of these kids as Trojan horses, or perhaps more accurately, Trojan ponies. They gallop into Washington and into our state legislatures with all that Obama-certified new wisdom to dispense. They demand that our invertebrate legislators surrender rights that Americans have held since before the Founding.

But their *new wisdom* looks suspiciously like the *old wisdom* of the gun grabbers—the warmed-over ideas we have heard whether the face of the gun control movement is Michael Bloomberg or James Brady or Gabrielle Giffords.

The whole anti-self-defense, anti-gun, anti-American agenda is here—again.

Only this time it's disguised as the "new wisdom" of high school students.

So, the Trojan ponies call for limiting magazine capacities, banning scary-looking rifles, and raising the minimum age to buy a gun to twenty-one.

That last point is ironic: *Please make me wait to buy a gun until I'm twenty-one because I'm not mature enough at eighteen, but listen to me about everything else because I'm seventeen and I "see the world anew."*

Of course, seeing the world *anew* is actually seeing an *old* world—the feudal world. A world where the peasantry is disarmed and the king controls the army—and all the arms.

You know that world from the movies. It's called *The Hunger Games*.

The Capitol gets the stormtroopers and rocket systems; the peasants get a bow and arrow, *if they're lucky*.

That's the *new* world these wise teens are hoping to inflict on all of us.

The famous environmental activist, novelist, and essayist Edward Abbey understood the consequences of this all too well. He said, "If guns are outlawed, only the government will have guns."

That's Michael Bloomberg's dream world.

If you think the young #NeverAgain oracles have much to teach us, take a look at some of the profound "arguments" they advance:

- "When your old-ass parent is like, 'I don't know how to send an iMessage,' and you're just like, 'Give me the fucking phone and let me handle it.' Sadly, that's what we have to do with our government; our parents don't know how to use a fucking democracy, so we have to."[20]

- "It just makes me think what sick fuckers out there want to continue to sell more guns, murder more children, and honestly just get reelected. What type of shitty person does that? They could have blood from children splattered all over their faces and they wouldn't take action, because they all still see these dollar signs."[21]

- "Go join the Army if you want to have fun shooting off a weapon, and serve your fucking country."[22]
- To Florida governor Rick Scott: "You're kind of like Voldemort at this point. You should just retire, because you aren't going to get elected to Senate."[23]
- To Benjamin Kelly, a former aide to State Representative Shawn Harrison, who accused Hogg of being a crisis actor: "Hey, if you're out there, fuck you."[24]

How any of this stops criminals and crazies from murdering us they don't explain, but when you're seventeen maybe you don't need to.

David Hogg and his fellow student activists may desire safety but they don't want to accept the fact that it's up to them to make smart decisions that will keep them safe. The anti-gun lobby is encouraging these kids to give up fundamental rights they have never had—or are even old enough to exercise. Foreclosing their options of how to protect themselves when they become adults doesn't really seem like all that smart a choice.

Of course, it's far easier to give up something you don't have than something you have.

What was Hogg's reaction when he learned that he was going to have to wear a clear backpack to school? Well, *that* was a bridge too far.[25] Suddenly his First

24

Amendment right to an opaque backpack was being violated.

You wanted more government, David; you got more government.

A Tried-and-True Tactic

The Parkland kids are far from the first sympathetic young people to be adopted to advance a political agenda.

Norma McCorvey was a desperate young woman in 1969 when she became pregnant for the third time.[26] A pair of Texas lawyers and other political activists were then seeking a sympathetic plaintiff to challenge state law on abortion.[27] They decided that Norma made a good choice.[28]

So, Norma McCorvey became known as the plaintiff Jane Roe, a name immortalized in American jurisprudence via the *Roe v. Wade* Supreme Court decision that declared abortion a right.[29]

Years later, McCorvey revealed that she had been used. The pro-abortion attorneys and activists "connected my name to a case that I never knew about in the beginning, never participated in, never believed in," she told an interviewer. "I was just a pawn."[30]

Pawns. It happens again and again. In fact, the technique of recruiting young people to advance a political agenda dates back to centuries before *Roe v. Wade*.

In the early thirteenth century, young people from throughout Europe were recruited to take part in the Crusades to expel Muslims from Jerusalem. This "Children's Crusade" is remembered for being led by visionaries and leaders as young as twelve. But many accounts were embellished, and in some cases unscrupulous merchants exploited the situation to sell young people into slavery.

The Parkland kids aren't being sold into slavery or marched thousands of miles to fight in a holy war. On the contrary, they are fêted everywhere. Prominent figures heap adulation on them. They appear on television and speak in front of massive, adoring crowds. What young person wouldn't be excited by such experiences? And good for them!

But it's a form of exploitation nonetheless. Gun control activists are using these kids to promote an agenda they have failed to enact previously. The young people being exploited today are not being used to advance freedom or expand rights. Instead, they are being used for the purpose of taking away the rights of people and eroding the protections of the Constitution. They are being told it is good to promote the diminution (and elimination) of their own constitutional rights.

From a political standpoint, children are ideal carriers of messages because they are unassailable, particularly if they have a direct connection to a tragedy. For the gun control movement, children represent a win-win-win. They are sympathetic, they are beyond reproach, and they cannot be challenged by anyone. These factors make children ripe for exploitation and explain why we see so many of them in the media today promoting gun control.

The "Expertise" of the Survivor

The Parkland students are especially powerful spokespeople because they are survivors. They survived an attack where a crazy person killed their friends and classmates. They fled in fear for their own lives. No one should have to endure such a terrifying experience. Mercifully, few of us ever will.

So, it made sense that news networks rushed to put David Hogg and his fellow Parkland students on the air after the shooting. Eyewitness accounts have long been a staple of news coverage of tragedies.

But does being a survivor bestow special credibility to speak as an expert on topics that the person otherwise knows very little about?

No, it doesn't.

This is not to diminish the ordeal the Parkland students went through. It's just a hard truth. Survival itself does not automatically make you a subject matter expert.

Surviving cancer doesn't turn you into a medical expert. Surviving a car crash doesn't make you a car safety expert. And surviving a shooting does not make you an expert on gun policy or the Bill of Rights.

Sorry, it just doesn't.

But the gun grabbers understand that many people grant the survivors of mass shootings a moral authority to speak. Anti-gun activists also know that, out of sympathy, most people won't forcefully challenge the survivors' views.

Chapter 2
Do As I Say, Not As I Do (Because I'm More Important Than You)

"Despite the fact that they often
speak of them with genuine
conviction, these do-as-I-say liberals
don't actually trust their ideas enough
to apply them at home. Instead, when
it comes to the things that matter
most in their personal lives, they tend
to behave—ironically—more like
conservatives than liberals. Which
can only make one wonder: If their
liberal prescriptions don't really work
for them as individuals, how can they
work for the rest of us?"
—Peter Schweizer, *Do As I Say (Not
As I Do): Profiles in Liberal Hypocrisy*

In his famous political novel *Animal Farm*, George
Orwell wrote, "All animals are equal, but some animals
are more equal than others." Orwell's quote could be
applied directly to the goals of America's elite gun
grabbers: All Americans should be equally disarmed, but
some Americans are special and are entitled to the
protection of guns.

29

Real life is not a Hollywood movie. In the real world, *Atomic Blonde* actress Charlize Theron can't take out half a dozen East German security agents, and superhero Scarlett Johansson can't beat up a man twice her size. When the latest protest march ends, many of the anti-gun hypocrites will go home to their well-guarded compounds or gated communities, and you will just go home. No armed guards and electric gates for you. And for those who may think they're "sticking it to the man" by begging politicians to take away your civil right of self-defense, the reality is that this is exactly what "the man" wants you to do. You are ensuring your own helplessness.

"In God we trust, all others must bring data," said W. Edwards Deming.[31] Guess what happens when you look at the available data about how the wealthiest, prettiest, and most famous among us choose to protect their lives.[32] It turns out these folks have a strong penchant for guns and bodyguards, all the while surrounding their fancy events with phalanxes of police officers.

Did you know Facebook spends $20,000 each day—$7.3 million every year—on security for Mark Zuckerberg?[33] At that price, do you think that security comes with a few handguns? But Zuckerberg doesn't want *you* to have guns.[34] Facebook's advertising rules state that "Ads must not promote the sale or use of weapons, ammunition or explosives."[35]

How about we look to the hypocrite celebrities, plutocrats, and politicians who are surrounded by legal armed mercenaries (known as their security details) but want you and your peers to give up your rights to defend yourself?

Want some other examples?[36] I will just hit the hypocritical highlights. Here are but a few celebrities who support more gun control yet have security details or bodyguards.

Hollywood Celebrities

At the 2018 Academy Awards, Hollywood's elite arranged for five hundred Los Angeles police officers to provide security, and that was just the beginning. *Variety* reported: "More than 500 officers will be on hand, many of them working overtime, to ensure the safety of the 90th Academy Awards, along with firefighters, police helicopters and agents from the FBI. Private security guards from Security Industry Specialists will work the inside of the theater."[37]

When the Grammy Awards were held at Madison Square Garden, the musical elite not only had the benefit of a massive police presence but also received free counterterrorism training from U.S. and European experts before the show.[38] I am sure you received the same free briefing on your way to the grocery store.

George Clooney was one of the first people to donate to the March for Our Lives ($500,000). Yet what does he do when it comes to his family's safety? Clooney, after the birth of his twins, spent oodles of money on protection for his family. *Marie Claire* magazine reported that the Clooneys "have invested in an increased security team, complete with a 24/7 guard service surrounding their LA, UK and Italian homes." The report continued: "But it doesn't stop there. The Clooneys are determined to keep their children safe, and have reportedly added video surveillance, bulletproof walls, panic rooms and basement bunkers to make sure that Alexander and Ella are kept away from danger."[39] That's right, folks, skip owning guns and just purchase your own 24/7 security team for your homes in Los Angeles, London, and Tuscany.

Other March for Our Lives supporters go all-out to protect themselves too. Oprah supports gun control for the peasants but has traveled with more than a dozen bodyguards on a single trip.[40] Steven Spielberg enjoys the benefits of security at home and on his movie sets.[41]

Kim Kardashian supports gun control but uses her multimillion-dollar fortune to hire 24/7-armed security.[42]

Sylvester Stallone of *Rambo* fame supports national gun control but has had bodyguards.[43]

Singer Ariana Grande wants gun control but benefits from bodyguards on tour.[44]

Jennifer Lawrence of *The Hunger Games* fame supports gun control but has a bodyguard.[45]

Lady Gaga supports gun control but uses bodyguards.[46]

Actress Kristen Stewart wants gun control but uses a bodyguard.[47]

Singer Selena Gomez supports gun control but uses a bodyguard.[48]

Britney Spears supports gun control but uses a bodyguard.[49]

Katy Perry too.[50]

Beyoncé too.[51]

Having learned her gun control hypocrisy from her cousin Senator Chuck Schumer (D-NY), comedian Amy Schumer went out and hired more security for herself when she feared for her safety.[52]

Alyssa Milano and Rosie O'Donnell used armed guards *at anti-gun rallies.*[53]

But in fairness and in contrast, I must compliment Brad Pitt and Angelia Jolie for being proud gun owners. Jolie declared: "If anybody comes into my home and tries to hurt my kids...I have no problem shooting them."[54]

At least someone in Hollywood has some common sense.

Billionaire Elites

Michael Bloomberg is a notorious hypocrite when it comes to gun issues. While spending millions supporting gun control as applied to the little people, Bloomberg surrounds himself with armed men everywhere he travels. Amusingly, then-Mayor Bloomberg would travel to gun-free Bermuda, where even the police do not carry guns, and what would Bloomberg bring with him (besides a bottle of Coppertone)? Twelve armed guards.[55] Wait, Bermuda has banned guns—so shouldn't it be the safest place in the world? Shouldn't Bloomberg have felt safe to go there without guns?

Comedian Jackie Mason once said this about Bloomberg's hypocrisy: "As if his life counts, but yours is not important? If guns are not important and nobody should have a gun to protect himself, why does Bloomberg have 12 bodyguards? Why doesn't he stand there with 12 rabbis? Why do they have guns? Instead of guns they should have pastrami sandwiches."[56]

Paul Allen, the billionaire owner of the NFL's Seattle Seahawks and the NBA's Portland Trailblazers, who made his riches from cofounding Microsoft with Bill Gates, donated one million dollars to gun control efforts in Washington State.[57] Allen is protected by an elite group of between eight and fourteen security contractors who travel with him and provide security for him.[58] Allen's private security detail includes former FBI agents and retired Navy SEALs—probably just like the guys protecting your home when you sleep.[59] Part of the work performed by these private guards includes protecting Allen's 414-foot yacht, called the *Octopus*.[60]

And there you see the hypocrisy and double standards so endemic to the gun grabbers. They want *you* to be disarmed because *you* are not special like them. They deserve to be protected with guns from bad people doing bad things, but we do not deserve the same rights and protections. Why? Because we simply aren't important enough.

Federal Government Elites

Washington politicians who support gun control get the benefit of armed guards—at the expense of the taxpayers. Former vice president Joe Biden not only received free Secret Service protection while in office, he actually made a financial profit off the arrangement.[61]

Barack and Michelle Obama both support gun control (perhaps to get Americans to stop "clinging to their guns and religion").[62] But President Obama did not hesitate to sign a law that guaranteed he and his wife would receive armed Secret Service protection for the rest of their lives.[63] Did he just like the company, or did he want their protection?

Hillary Rodham Clinton gets lifetime Secret Service protection paid for by the American taxpayer. A small fortune was spent protecting her home in Chappaqua, New York, including by building a large surrounding wall.[64] (Walls in Chappaqua but not at the border!)

In 2015, armed guards protected Democratic senators as they demanded more gun control.[65] Senator Dianne Feinstein (D-CA), a proponent of the 1994 "assault weapon" ban, admitted to previously holding concealed-carry permits.[66] Of course, Senator Feinstein is now married to a successful investment banker and has a net worth of $42 million.[67] So it is fair to say she can afford her own security guards.

In a 2017 article about Secret Service protection,[68] *The New York Times* reported:

- The U.S. Secretary of Commerce enjoys bodyguards when he attends fancy dinners.
- When congressmen attend baseball practice, they get the benefit of armed guards.
- U.S. Supreme Court justices often receive armed protection when traveling outside of Washington.
- The Environmental Protection Agency requested funds to form a twenty-four-hour security detail for its current administrator, adding ten full-time staff members.
- The Secretary of Transportation is protected by the department's Office of Intelligence, Security, and Emergency Response.
- The Senate majority leader receives 24/7 protection by the Capitol Police.
- The Secretary of Agriculture has a protective detail, as does the Secretary of Housing and Urban Development.
- The head of the Department of Veterans Affairs is protected during travel, public events, and visits, while also receiving transportation to and from work.

And, of course, all of Congress receives 24/7-armed protection on Capitol Hill.[69]

In the immortal words of Dana Carvey's Church Lady character on *Saturday Night Live*, "Well, isn't that special."

Royal Elites

The day after the royal wedding of Prince Harry and Meghan Markle, the cover of the *New York Daily News* read: "They do royal weddings. We do schoolkids' funerals."[70]

The cover story writers for the rabidly anti-gun *Daily News* probably thought they were being clever. In reality, the headline proved the hypocrisy.

The Santa Fe, Texas, shooting victims died in a virtually gun-free zone where their teachers were unarmed.[71] Unlike the *hoi polloi* students in Texas, the royal couple and their guests, which included George Clooney and Oprah, were surrounded by countless good guys with guns (snipers and undercover cops) and counter-UAV systems.[72] The cost of the royal wedding was approximately $42 million; *94 percent* of that figure was spent on security.[73] Go figure.

Religious Elites

Let's turn to the religious elite.

Pope Francis lectures us on gun control from behind his walled fortress (Vatican City) surrounded by his small, but deadly, force of special ops soldiers known as the Swiss Guard. The Pope is one of the most heavily guarded people in the world.[74]

Many leaders in the Catholic Church support gun control.[75] Yet these leaders also enjoy the benefit of armed protection, including, on occasion, heavily armed police officers.[76]

The Long Con

The gun grabbers' game is simply a con. Tell them to get rid of their bodyguards first. When they speak about gun control, what they're really saying to you is: "Guns for me, but not for thee."

Tell those anti-gun hypocrites rich enough to hire their own security teams:

"You disarm first."

Part 2

Your Intellectual Ammunition: Exposing the Gun Grabbers' Favorite Myths

With the deep political divide and heightened passions these days, it's hard to have a serious discussion about complicated issues. And it's almost impossible to do so when any discussion of facts is ruled off-limits, as it has been in the gun debate. All we hear are soundbites and appeals to emotion: "Never again!" "Do something!" "We have to stop this!" "F*** the NRA!"

But facts are stubborn things.

Here I will expose the false arguments the gun grabbers use and the inconvenient truths they fail to mention.

Chapter 3
Gun Grabber Myth #1
"Nobody Needs a Gun"

The gun grabbers say: "Why does anyone need a gun?"

The truth: God made man, but Sam Colt made them equal.

"Be not afraid of any man,
No matter what his size,
When danger threatens, call on me –
And I will equalize!"
—A poem about the Colt
Peacemaker revolver[77]

How is it that so many kids raised on *Harry Potter*, *The Hunger Games*, *Star Wars*, and all the Marvel action figure movies manage to miss a critical point of the stories? The lesson being: If you want to prevail over evil villains, you must have the proper tools to fight back.

Millions of people in the U.S. have guns to protect themselves and their families. They choose guns as a means of self-defense for the same reason the Secret Service uses them to protect the president: guns stop bad people from doing bad things to good people.

It's absurd to speak about the right of self-defense in theory but then deny people the tools they need to exercise that right. It would be like appearing on a cooking show without knives. Life shouldn't be like an episode of *Naked and Afraid*.

You might choose not to own a firearm, but there is no denying that each of us has an inalienable right to self-defense. It should, in fact, be one of the most preciously guarded in the panoply of American rights. After all, the right to self-defense protects the most fundamental right of all—the right to life—and is the shield for all our other rights.

Without a gun, most Americans are defenseless at the hands of a violent criminal. How many of us have training in hand-to-hand fighting, the physical strength, and the mental resilience to react in a fight-or-flight situation to repel an aggressive predator, especially someone who attacks us first and is armed with a deadly weapon?

Remember, you can't attend the Women's March, enjoy Bravo's *Watch What Happens Live with Andy Cohen,* or listen to National Public Radio if you're dead. If we can't protect ourselves, we are left vulnerable to the predators, violent criminals, and mentally unstable individuals prowling our streets.

Without the right and the means to self-defense, your right to life has no meaning. Not a pleasant thought, but that is why I've written this book: to get people to face the unpleasant thought that anyone, anywhere, might be a victim and that having the means to fight back immediately is the best option.

Let's not kid ourselves: the world is dangerous. Just glance at the news and you'll see street crimes, mob violence, gangs of illegal aliens (MS-13, anyone?), and psychopaths engaging in unspeakable acts of horror. Saying "it won't happen to me" is not a life plan—it is naive and dangerous.

You never know when evil will appear. It comes at inconvenient times. The aggressor picks *his* time to attack; *you* won't be consulted.

Where defending your life is concerned, you're going to need more than your morning mantras if you hope to come out the victor. Telling yourself "I am fierce" and "I can be anything I want" will probably get you killed (or at least seriously injured) when you're confronted by a violent or crazy attacker.

That's not a message aimed exclusively at women, by the way. Men are more likely than women to experience violence in the United States.[78] If you're a man, you need to be prepared.

And if you're a woman, you need to be prepared too. Telling yourself stories like, "I'm no one's prey" and "I can kick his a**" may be tempting. After all, you've seen *Revenge, Black Widow*, and *The Hunger Games*. But even if the underdog always prevails in those movies (and in the *James Bond* films), triumphing over a couple of two-hundred-pound male attackers in real life takes more than a great script. Believing in soothing stories, aka fairytales, can get you killed.

In the real world, the ill-equipped and underprepared underdog is rarely going to win.

Does a gun guarantee your safety? No, but it gives you the ability to defend yourself against an armed, physically superior, or mentally unstable attacker (or all three). A gun is the great equalizer, as the poem at the beginning of the chapter reminds us.

Why in the world would anyone *not* want to have the means to protect themselves and their families against criminal predators and lunatics? Worse yet, why would anyone actively lobby their government to deprive themselves and every other law-abiding citizen of the most effective means to protect themselves?

Some people won't consider carrying a gun for self-defense because thinking about yourself as a potential victim is fundamentally unpleasant. It's like thinking about getting cancer. No thanks.

If you choose not to avail yourself of a gun for personal defense, you have made a choice for yourself, like ignoring the risk of a two-pack-a-day cigarette habit. But how can you morally impose your will on your family, friends, and neighbors? How can you deny the rest of us the right to defend ourselves and our families? Are you going to guarantee my safety?

The gun grabbers are convinced that if we shut down the NRA and take away guns from law-abiding gun owners, then bad people will no longer have the tools to do bad things. I don't know about you, but I stopped believing in unicorns and leprechauns when I stopped believing in Santa Claus, the Easter Bunny, and the Tooth Fairy. For reasons you'll see in the chapters ahead, even the most restrictive gun laws don't stop determined killers.

A gun is a tool, plain and simple. You should own a gun for the same reason you install smoke and carbon monoxide detectors, purchase fire extinguishers, and buckle your seat belt. An ounce of prevention is worth a pound of cure.

Smart people are prepared. Foolish people bring a knife—or nothing at all—to a gunfight.

The gun grabbers say: "There is no evidence that guns save lives."

The truth: If there is no proof that guns save lives, then why does every American law enforcement agency, including the U.S. Secret Service, carry guns? What's the point of the guns?

There is an old saying in the world of investing: "Do what the smart money does." This means that when you personally invest, it makes sense to buy and sell the same investments as the "smart money" people—large banks, institutional investors, hedge funds, and investment gurus like Warren Buffett. The idea is that these industry leaders have a better understanding of the marketplace and better access to information than ordinary investors do. And that is usually true.

What do the "smart money" people do when it comes to protecting lives?

Virtually all professionals carry guns—and lots of them. Federal, state, and local law enforcement agencies charged with protecting the streets you walk on all carry guns. The Secret Service protects the president with guns. The federal Department of Homeland Security, with its $44 billion annual budget, issues its own agents handguns and fully automatic rifles (rifles far more powerful than the AR-15s many gun grabbers don't want you to have to protect yourself).

So, the smart money in the business of protecting lives chooses guns. That's right. They choose guns!

Remember those old toothpaste ads that said, "Nine out of ten dentists recommend Crest"? Well, ten out of ten U.S. law enforcement agencies choose to carry firearms.

But if you don't want to follow the smart money on guns, then let's turn to the statistical scoreboard. Does civilian gun use help in self-defense against criminals?

The U.S. Department of Justice investigated firearm violence from 1993 through 2011.[79] The report found, "In 2007–2011, about 1% of nonfatal violent crime victims used a firearm in self-defense."[80] Anti-gun zealots attempt to use this statistic to discredit the use of a gun as a viable means of self-defense, and by extension, to discredit gun ownership in general.

But look deeper into the numbers. During that five-year period, the Department of Justice confirmed a total of 338,700 defensive gun uses in both violent attacks and property crimes where a victim was involved. That equals an average of *67,740 defensive gun uses every year*. In other words, according to the Justice Department's own statistics, *67,740* people a year don't become victims because they own a gun. (I suspect that if more states allowed concealed carry to be widespread, the number of instances of defensive gun uses would be even higher.)

Is it significant that at least 67,740 individuals use a gun in self-defense each year? Well, in 2016, 37,461 people died in motor vehicle accidents in the United States. In 2015, the number was 35,092 people.[81] Mark Rosekind, administrator of the National Highway Transportation and Safety Administration (NHTSA), called those road fatalities "an immediate crisis."[82] If the NHTSA administrator considers it a crisis that approximately 37,000 people are dying annually from car accidents, then *saving* nearly twice that many people each year through the use of firearms is simply stunning.

In reality, the Department of Justice findings about defensive gun uses are very conservative. A 2013 study ordered by the Centers for Disease Control and Prevention (CDC) and conducted by the Institute of Medicine and the National Research Council found that "Defensive use of guns by crime victims is a common occurrence....Almost all national survey estimates indicate that defensive gun uses by victims are at least as common as offensive uses by criminals, with estimates of annual uses ranging from about 500,000 to more than 3 million...in the context of about 300,000 violent crimes involving firearms in 2008.... On the other hand, some scholars point to a radically lower estimate of only 108,000 annual defensive uses based on the National Crime Victimization Survey...." [83]

The most comprehensive study ever conducted about defensive gun use in the United States was a 1995 survey published by criminologist Gary Kleck in the *Journal of Criminal Law and Criminology*. This study reported between 2.1 and 2.5 million defensive gun uses every year. [84]

The gun grabbers have spent a lot of time (and money) trying to debunk Kleck's study. The CDC apparently undertook a three-year study in at least fifteen states to refute the findings on defensive gun uses. [85] From 1996 to 1998, the CDC asked respondents, "During the last 12 months, have you confronted another person with a firearm, even if you did not fire it, to protect yourself, your property, or someone else?" [86]

But the CDC, with its $11 billion annual budget, never published its findings and never even publicly acknowledged that its surveys asked the question.[87]

Why not? Kleck unearthed the CDC's lost data two decades later.[88] Although Kleck is reviewing this CDC data to determine how, if at all, this data may influence his previous research, a preliminary review of the data suggests that it may reflect findings consistent with Kleck's previous conclusions.[89]

The CDC has made its anti-gun views well known. Dr. Mark Rosenberg, who led the CDC's gun research in the 1990s, said: "We need to revolutionize the way we look at guns, like what we did with cigarettes. It used to be that smoking was a glamour symbol, cool, sexy, macho. Now it is dirty, deadly, and banned."[90]

Ultimately, the number of defensive gun uses doesn't matter much to the anti-gun zealots. Whether the number is 67,000 or 2.5 million or anywhere in between, they'll do whatever they can to dismiss defensive gun uses as insignificant. They want to focus only on the dead people lying in the street rather than those folks who use a firearm to remain standing. I suspect those people still alive would have a different view!

Ask anyone who has defended his or her life with a gun. You can ask Ethel Jones, the sixty-nine-year-old woman who shot an eighteen-year-old male who broke into her home and entered her bedroom at 3 a.m.[91] Or ask the owner of the Peking Restaurant in Bridgeport,

Connecticut, who used his gun to force two armed robbers to flee.[92] Or ask the owner of the Alabama bait shop who used a gun to defend himself when a career criminal tried to rob his store.[93] And so on and so on.

The gun grabbers want us to believe that by taking away the ability of those people to defend themselves, they are making society safer. But America is relatively safe. All they are doing is belittling the victims and their right to self-defense. Keep in mind, there are *many* victims. According to recent FBI statistics, in 2016 there were 1.2 million violent crimes in the United States, including 771,000 aggravated assaults and 95,730 rapes.[94] Those are rapes and assaults that might have been thwarted had the victims been armed and able to protect themselves.

Ultimately, we don't need numbers to justify the right to self-defense. Liberals often set the standard at one. President Barack Obama explained, "If we save even one life from gun violence, it's worth it."[95] Let's adopt the "just one" standard too. If just one person can defend his or her life or liberty with a gun, it's worth it.

The gun grabbers say: "Good guys with guns don't stop mass shootings."

The truth: Good guys with guns save lives more often than the media want us to think.

Guns aren't the answer. That's what the people who hate guns tell us. The gun grabbers treat gun-rights advocates the way atheists treat the devout: they look down on them, shocked that they could believe in such a thing.

But when you look at FBI statistics, you'll see that pro-gun people's views aren't based on fairy tales.

In a May 2018 report,[96] the FBI analyzed the fifty active-shooter incidents that took place in 2016 and 2017, twenty of which qualified as mass shootings. They found that in four active-shooter incidents, citizens with valid gun permits successfully stopped the shooter.[97] The FBI reported that "In four incidents, citizens possessing valid firearms permits successfully stopped the shooter. In two incidents, citizens exchanged gunfire with the shooter. In two incidents, the citizens held the shooter at gunpoint until law enforcement arrived."[98]

In each of those four incidents, brave citizens legally possessing a gun risked their own safety to save others' lives:

- **September 28, 2016, Townville, South Carolina:** A teen with a gun began shooting at an elementary school playground after killing his father at their home.[99] Jamie Brock, a volunteer firefighter with a valid firearms permit, held the shooter until police arrived.[100]

- **September 24, 2017, Antioch, Tennessee:** A gunman opened fire in the parking lot of the Burnette Chapel Church of Christ.[101] Robert Engle, who had a valid firearms permit, ran to his car to retrieve his gun and then held the shooter at gunpoint until the police arrived.[102]

- **November 5, 2017, Sutherland Springs, Texas:** Stephen Willeford confronted a shooter who had killed twenty-six people at a local church.[103] Willeford chased the shooter, fired at the shooter with the AR-15 he had in his truck, and brought an end to the killing spree.[104]

- **November 17, 2017, Rockledge, Florida:** A gunman began shooting in the parking lot of Schlenker Automotive.[105] Two people working at the shop had valid permits and exchanged gunfire with the killer.[106] Their bravery halted the attack and held off the gunman until police arrived.[107]

There were also two additional incidents in which armed citizens tried to intervene but were unsuccessful.[108] But that is not a failure of the right to carry. Where armed citizens were able to intervene, they succeeded in reducing or preventing casualties in four out of six instances, or 67 percent of the time.

Ultimately, active shooters met armed resistance from citizens six times out of fifty.[109] That's 12 percent of the time.

And these numbers underestimate the value of a fully armed citizen. Many times, an armed citizen thwarts a criminal *before* the criminal can become an active shooter. In May 2018, a nineteen-year-old shooter entered a northern Illinois high school where students had gathered for graduation rehearsal and began to fire.[110] A school resource officer, Mark Dallas, heard the shots and responded. He exchanged fire with the shooter, eventually injuring the gunman and ending the conflict.[111] The gunman suffered the only injury and the resource officer was hailed as a hero for saving many lives.

Good guys with guns have been credited with saving multiple lives all over this great nation. Here are some more examples:[112]

- at a Baptist church in Boiling Springs, South Carolina, a gunman was held at gunpoint by the reverend's son, Aaron Guyton, before he could open fire on the congregation (2012).[113]
- at a sports bar in Arlington, Texas, a gunman was shot dead by a patron after killing the bar manager and before he could harm others. Use of force and firearms expert Emanuel Kapelsohn told NBC News, "Who

knows how many people would be dead if he had not acted?" (2017)[114]

- at a nightclub in Lyman, South Carolina, a shooter who opened fire injuring three was shot in the leg by a club patron who had a valid concealed carry permit and was found to be acting in self-defense. (2016)[115]

- at a liquor store in Conyers, Georgia, a killing spree was cut short by Todd Scott, who returned fire when a man entered the store and began shooting, killing two patrons. Rockdale County Sheriff Eric Levett told the press that Scott "very likely prevented other customers in the store from losing their lives." (2015)[116]

- at a hospital in Darby, Pennsylvania, Dr. Lee Silverman shot a felon and psychiatric patient who had just shot and killed his case worker. Silverman was also grazed by a bullet. While it is against hospital policy for anyone other than security to carry a firearm, Dr. Silverman was credited by Donald Molineux, chief of the Yeadon Police Department, saying he "without a doubt saved lives." (2014)[117]

- at a strip club in Portland, Oregon, a repeat felon who opened fire in the club was stopped when bouncer Jonathan Baer returned fire and ended the attack (2014).[118]

We don't hear much about any of this. When a citizen does get media attention for thwarting a criminal, it is often because he is an *unarmed* citizen.

Let's compare two incidents that occurred in April 2018, both in Waffle House restaurants.

The mainstream media heaped praise on an unarmed man who rushed the shooter at a Waffle House in Antioch, Tennessee. That brave man no doubt deserves accolades, but the mainstream media ignored another man who thwarted armed robbers at a Waffle House in New Orleans by drawing his gun and firing.[119]

The number of people killed in the first incident? Four. The number killed in the second? Zero.

Media bias against guns? You betcha!

Unarmed citizens who confront criminals should be saluted for their bravery. But wouldn't they be far better off if they had guns? Soldiers storming the beaches of Normandy in 1944 would have been very brave to attack Nazi bunkers armed with nothing more than a canteen; of course, they were far more effective having guns. And that 2013 CDC report agrees, "Studies that directly assessed the effect of actual defensive uses of guns (*i.e.*, incidents in which a gun was "used" by the crime victim in the sense of attacking or threatening an offender) have found consistently lower injury rates among gun-using crime victims compared with victims who used other self-protective strategies."[120]

Just as we salute unarmed citizens for confronting evil, we should also salute *armed* citizens for doing the same. However, the media want you to believe that guns are evil with no redeeming purpose. So instead they ignore the facts inconsistent with the story they want to sell you.

The facts tell the real story. Guns work. Guns save lives. The only thing that limits the effectiveness of good guys with guns in stopping bad guys with guns is the limited number of good guys with guns.

Chapter 4
Gun Grabber Myth #2
"You don't need a gun. Highly trained government professionals are here to protect you."

Wait, so you trust police and government now? What happened to "Hands Up, Don't Shoot"?

The gun grabbers say: "Leave the guns to the trained first responders."

The truth: You are your own first responder.

Economist Milton Friedman once explained that there are two types of money: your money and everyone else's. You spend your money carefully and wisely. You spend other people's money with less care.[121]

The same logic applies when it comes to protecting lives. Mostly, people will be more protective of their own lives and the lives of their family than they will be with the lives of others. Just look at any mother lion; she may make some noise if the pride is threatened, but if you threaten her cubs, you will be met with a fierce attack.

Or think back to all those celebrities who line up to oppose gun rights even as they protect themselves and their families with armed guards. Those celebrities are guilty of hypocrisy, sure. But they're not so foolish or misguided not to adequately defend *themselves*.

If you don't see to your own self-defense, who will protect you? If you don't protect your family, who will? The government? The police?

Don't count on it.

I respect police officers. But think about the term *first responders*. Police are supposedly the first to *respond* to a crime or dangerous situation. But in most cases, police arrive on the scene *after* the crime has been committed, *after* the people targeted have been victimized, and *after* the bad guys run away. They are almost always after-event actors. This is not their fault; it is the nature of policing.

Who is the *real* first responder? That's easy: it's the intended victim of a violent crime.

That could be you. How would you respond to a threat against your life?

You can take one of any number of approaches. You could take a Gandhi-like approach of passive resistance (and hope your enemy is more like the civilized Brits than the Nazis).[122] You can accept that violence is inevitable and submit. Or you can try to fight back.

58

Many say that it's better to die on your feet than live on your knees. If this is your view of life, then guns are your friend.

You also have the right to choose to call 911, hide in a closet, and hope for the best. But understand that this is not being prepared.

And for many victims, law enforcement's best isn't good enough.

Recently a Texas 911 phone operator was sentenced to jail time for "systematically" hanging up on *thousands* of 911 calls, including an attempt to report a violent burglary.[123]

Or look at the school shootings in Parkland, Florida, in February 2018. The Broward County Sheriff's Department had already stationed a deputy at the high school.[124] The department's rules of engagement required the deputy, Scot Peterson, to enter the school to confront the shooter.[125]

Peterson didn't do that. When students began fleeing from the campus, he radioed to make sure "no one comes inside the school."[126]

Officer Peterson screwed up badly enough that he resigned in disgrace.[127] But can you really expect a low-paid government employee (or even a highly paid one) to risk his life to save yours? I'm not taking that bet.

Peterson's mistake wasn't the government's first failure to deal with the killer, Nikolas Cruz. Broward County police failed to act in dozens of interactions with this extremely troubled youth, until he finally went over the edge and embarked on a killing spree. And the school district failed too.[128]

Let's consider some other high-profile shootings from recent years:

Columbine: This was another failure of law enforcement. The shooters already had a history with the authorities, having served time in a juvenile diversion program the year before.[129] They made threats about killing a fellow student, including posting those threats on the internet.[130] And they posted information online that they had pipe bombs and a hit list of people to kill.[131] Jefferson County Sheriff investigator Michael Guerra also discovered a variety of threats against Columbine teachers and students.[132]

Guerra drafted an affidavit in pursuit of a search warrant, but the affidavit was never filed.[133] Had the search warrant been executed—the affidavit was drafted months before the shooting—it's entirely possible that the tragedy would not have occurred. Instead that case was forgotten.

Forgotten until April 20, 1999, when the two killers walked into their school and began shooting. People called 911 and law enforcement dispatched SWAT teams. But within thirteen minutes, twelve students and one teacher had been killed and twenty-three people wounded.[134] Instead of rushing in to save lives, SWAT took forty-seven minutes to enter the school, finally entering the building just when the shooters were taking their own lives.[135]

The failure was astounding, prompting the FBI to conduct a comprehensive review of the police response to the situation.[136] This was when the term *active shooter* first entered our lexicon.

This was said to be a seminal moment for police tactics. A new approach was supposed to save lives by having the first responders move in more quickly. But that hasn't worked out so well.

San Bernardino: Fast-forward to 2015. Two jihad-loving terrorists, a husband and wife, opened fire in the Inland Regional Center in San Bernardino, California, killing fourteen people and wounding twenty-one.[137]

Somehow the killers had escaped the attention of law enforcement and the intelligence community, even though they spent years proclaiming their wish for jihad during their online courting ritual.[138] They eventually married and began hatching their terror plot while amassing an assortment of weapons and ammunition.[139] The FBI found that the couple "were actually radicalized before they started courting or dating each other online, and online as early as the end of 2013, they were talking to each other about jihad and martyrdom before they became engaged and then married and lived together in the United States."[140] But when Tashfeen Malik applied to join her fiancé in the United States, the U.S. State Department did not ask her about her jihadist views.[141]

The authorities missed all these activities while allowing Malik to immigrate to the U.S., apparently to perform the mass murders Americans are unwilling to perform themselves.[142]

Police arrived at the Inland Regional Center on December 2, 2015, approximately three and a half minutes after the first 911 call was received.[143] But responding officers were unacquainted with one another and had to form ad hoc teams to respond using their active shooter training.[144] Two teams entered the building from opposite sides, but the terrorists escaped without the first responders seeing them.[145]

Four hours later—that is not a typo—*four hours* later, the police found and killed the killers.[146]

Pulse nightclub: The shooter, Omar Mir Seddique Mateen, was an admitted Islamic terrorist whom the FBI had investigated in 2013 and 2014 after he claimed ties both to al-Qaeda and Hezbollah.[147] In spite of his broadcasting his intentions far and wide, the shooter was merely placed on a watch list.[148] Once again, authorities missed all the early signs and red flags.

On June 12, 2016, he entered the Pulse nightclub in Orlando, Florida, and started shooting. The night ended with forty-nine dead, fifty-three injured, and the killer barricaded in the nightclub with hostages.[149]

Although police initially exchanged gunfire with Mateen, they were ordered to withdraw. Orlando SWAT then waited *three hours* (again, not a typo)—

that's right, *three hours*—before they entered the nightclub to confront the killer.[150]

Because police waited hours to enter the building, injured victims lay dying in the nightclub while texting friends and police for help. Emergency medical personnel did not enter the club to treat victims because it was deemed too dangerous. "At least five people who were alive in the bathrooms when the standoff began ultimately died at the club, witnesses and relatives said."[151] "They took too damn long for me," said Tiara Parker, 21, who was inside the bathroom. "If they had moved faster, they would have gotten us out of there and everybody could have possibly lived."[152]

Months following the Pulse nightclub shooting, these same officers were recognized for their valor and bravery.[153]

Mandalay Bay: How long did it take Las Vegas police officers to storm into the room at the Mandalay Bay Resort and Casino where gunman Stephen Paddock was laying down fire on a crowd of twenty-two thousand helpless concertgoers? It took 72 minutes between the time the initial shots were fired and when the police breached the shooter's hotel room.[154] The shooting left fifty-eight people dead and nearly five hundred injured.[155]

Santa Fe, Texas: Even when police respond with speed often the time between the start of the attack and the arrival of the police can be a matter of life or death.

According to the Galveston sheriff, officers responding to the Santa Fe shooting entered the high school and engaged the shooter "within four minutes" of him opening fire on classmates.[156] Sadly, all twenty-three of his victims were killed or wounded within that *4-minute period* before law enforcement arrived."[157] The police and the shooter exchanged fire thereafter for twenty-five minutes before the shooter gave himself up.[158]

Sandy Hook, Connecticut: It took less than three minutes for police to arrive on the scene of the Sandy Hook shooting.[159] That was certainly fast. Yet Adam Lanza killed twenty students and six teachers before taking his own life as the police approached.[160]

Robert Farago wrote on *The Truth About Guns* website that, "The bumper sticker version of the pro-gun position: when seconds count the police are only minutes away. Here's the thing: it's true. Even when highly trained police response teams are ready to rock and roll, they can't intervene fast enough to stop the killing."[161]

Unfortunately, the Sandy Hook murders prove this exact point.

Don't be misled by the famous police motto "To Protect and to Serve." Neither the police nor any other government official or agency has a legal responsibility to protect citizens. The U.S. Supreme Court has confirmed this in the cases *Castle Rock v. Gonzalez* and *DeShaney v. Winnebago County Department of Social Services.*

Does it really make sense to put all your faith in law enforcement? Police officers typically mean well, but the reality is that they work for the government and thus enjoy the benefits of sovereign immunity, which means you can't sue them (really). Nobody will be losing their pensions and, if there is a finding of liability and an award of damages, then the local taxpayers will usually foot the bill. This is in stark contrast to businesses that mess up and go belly up. Just look at the spectacular demise of the private business *Gawker*, one wrong internet post and poof—they are toast.[162]

How *could* law enforcement be legally responsible for the safety of every American? It simply is not possible for police to protect every citizen. If they were responsible, they would be sued over every criminal act.

Civil rights lawyer and criminologist Don B. Kates Jr. explained: "Even if all 500,000 American police officers were assigned to patrol, they could not protect 240 million citizens from upwards of 10 million criminals who enjoy the luxury of deciding when and where to strike. But we have nothing like 500,000 patrol officers; to determine how many police are actually available for any one shift, we must divide the 500,000 by four (three shifts per day, plus officers who have days off, are on sick leave, etc.). The resulting number must be cut in half to account for officers assigned to investigations, juvenile, records, laboratory, traffic, etc., rather than patrol."[163]

Some prominent gun grabbers don't trust the police, but for different reasons. Black Lives Matter and the National Action Network, the two leading radical anti-police social justice organizations, fully supported the March for Our Lives. They sent busloads of young people to join the demonstrations.[164]

Black Lives Matter aims to restrict the police from enforcing the most basic laws in areas like marijuana, disorderly conduct, trespassing, and public consumption of alcohol.[165] It also wants to ban police interaction with suspected lawbreakers when that interaction is based on the person's immigration status, furtive movements (such as acting nervous), being in a high-crime area, or resemblance to the description of a suspect.[166] Apparently, Black Lives Matter wants to stop the police from engaging in any kind of actual policing, short of the bad guy walking up to them and introducing himself as a criminal.[167]

Black Lives Matter supporters demonize police too. Here are some of the more telling signs seen at Black Lives Matter protests:

Real Terrorists Wear Badges
Oink Oink, Bang Bang

Dear Pigs: What Goes Around Comes Around
F**k the Police
Prisons Are Slavery, Police Are the Slave Trade
Abolish the Police, Smash the State, Liberate the HOOD!
Demilitarize the Police

If average Americans can't be trusted to own guns to protect themselves, and we can't trust the police because they are racist or otherwise evil, then whom do we trust to carry guns to fight the bad guys?

It seems the March for Our Lives activists have not given much thought to that. But the radicals at Black Lives Matter have thought about it, and their answer is clear: No one.

In the end, if you are fine letting police officers carry guns and put themselves into harm's way to protect your life, then shouldn't you also be willing to consider owning a gun to protect your life—especially where you have a greater incentive to save your own life than some stranger in a blue uniform?

The gun grabbers say: "We can trust the mental health professionals and the criminal justice system to protect us."

The truth: Guess who is coming to dinner? The criminals, cartels, caliphate fanatics, and the crazies!

Americans are very lucky for many reasons. We live in the freest and most prosperous country in the history of the Earth. But American life is fraught with dangers. We walk the same streets as a number of potentially violent predators. I call these threats the four Cs: common criminals, cartels (MS-13), caliphate fanatics (Islamic terrorists), and the crazies.

Harsh language? Politically incorrect? Maybe, but it shouldn't matter when questions of life and death are on the table.

Our country has suffered violent attacks in many ways from the activities of common criminals with high recidivism rates, to illegal immigrant crime cartels such as the ten-thousand-member-strong MS-13 and the fifty-thousand-member Latin Kings, to Islamic terrorists in waiting who seek the promise of a new Islamic state (called a caliphate) governed by Sharia law (9/11 anyone?). These criminals and terrorists operate daily on our streets and the police carry guns and wear bulletproof vests to protect themselves from the potential dangers posed by these groups.

But some of the highest-profile violent attacks come from the fourth category, which is the crazies.

When you look at mass killings of strangers—the horrifying incidents that spark the loudest cries for gun control—the reality is that many of the killers were obviously mentally ill. According to one study cited by the Heritage Foundation, 60 percent of mass public shooters have been diagnosed with a mental disorder or demonstrated signs of serious mental illness prior to the attack.[168]

Let's look at some recent mass murders:

Sandy Hook shooter Adam Lanza: Lanza suffered from serious and untreated mental illness.[169] When he was in the ninth grade, the Yale University Child Study Center recommended that he take medication and undergo "extensive special education supports, ongoing expert consultation and rigorous therapeutic supports."[170] These recommendations went largely ignored. Dr. Harold Schwartz, chief psychiatrist at Hartford Hospital's Institute of Living, concluded that "It was [Lanza's] untreated mental illness that was a predisposing factor" in this tragedy.[171] After he killed his mother on December 14, 2012, Lanza killed twenty elementary school students and six teachers before taking his own life.[172]

Parkland shooter Nikolas Cruz: In 2014, Cruz left Westglades Middle School in the eighth grade and enrolled in a school that offered psychiatric and other clinical services on campus.[173] In 2016, the Florida Department of Children and Families opened a case on Cruz, calling him "a vulnerable adult due to mental illness."[174] The report noted that Cruz said he planned to buy a gun, but "it is unknown what he is buying the gun for."[175] After two months, the department closed its case on Cruz, saying his "final level of risk is low" because he was taking medication regularly.[176] But the report stated that Cruz suffered from depression, ADHD, and autism.[177]

Isla Vista/UC Santa Barbara attacker Elliot Rodger: This twenty-two-year-old killed six people and wounded thirteen others in May 2014 before turning the gun on himself.[178] His own father said his son was "very mentally ill."[179] The Santa Barbara Sheriff's Office released a report on the shooting that documented Rodger's long history of mental illness.[180]

Aurora, Colorado, theater shooter James Holmes: During Holmes's trial, the court-appointed psychiatrist judged the shooter legally sane when he killed twelve people and injured fifty-eight others in July 2012.[181] But by that the doctor meant only that Holmes knew right from wrong.[182] The psychiatrist, Dr. Jeffrey Metzner, also said that Holmes's "mental illness led him to open fire," according to the Associated Press.[183] Dr. Metzner diagnosed Holmes with schizoaffective disorder.[184] He said Holmes's actions were "directly related" to delusions that killing people would increase his self-worth.[185]

Under *existing laws*, at least some of these killers should not have been able to own or possess firearms.[186] "Possession of a firearm by the mentally ill is regulated by both state and federal laws."[187] So the issue is not guns per se or the laws already on the books; it's about mental illness and how effectively we deal with the threat it poses. If we cannot honestly deal with that problem, then we are never going to seriously address the problem of mass shootings.

If you want public safety, don't think banning guns will help. Especially not when the government is doing so little to keep you safe from the threats they already know exist.

Did you know that half of all Americans live in a sanctuary for illegal aliens, some of whom may be criminals?[188] Some 564 state and municipal governments are sanctuaries.

Think about that: more than five hundred government bodies have said to their citizens—the legal and law-abiding ones—you don't matter, and your safety is not our responsibility.

It's the same principle with gun control. Your safety is secondary to the #NeverAgain agenda and their dream of a gun-free world. Sound familiar? It should, it's been the beginning of every dystopian story ever written and every effort to create governments run by the "really smart" people who know best how we should live our lives but end up killing large numbers of their population to get people to follow them.

It's the Anakin Skywalker approach to democracy. In *Star Wars: Attack of the Clones*, a young Anakin insists, "We need a system where the politicians sit down and discuss the problem, agree what's in the best interests of the people, and then do it." But his love, Padme, informs him that the problem is that the people don't always agree—"in fact, they hardly ever do." Anakin responds with a youthfully ignorant, "Then they should be made to."

This is what we are ultimately fighting against: people who think they know best and are going to make us follow them. Our safety is secondary to what they think society needs.

Chapter 5
Gun Grabber Myth #3
"Guns Are the Problem" But Somehow Other Instruments of Violence Are Not

The gun grabbers say: "We must do something about gun violence."

The truth: There is no such thing as "gun violence." It's a propaganda term.

Why is it that when it comes to guns, liberal pundits love to place the blame for murder on the *instrument* of murder but not on the murderer? It's like blaming the internet for child porn.

Guns are wrongly singled out over knives, cars, bats, and other instruments, as if guns possess a consciousness of their own like the cursed kitchenware in Disney's *Beauty and Beast.*

When marchers march and students protest, it's the guns that get the blame, as if there is a special cause for gun violence unrelated to just regular violence. Just look at some of the signs from the March for Our Lives:

> "Our Lives Are Worth More than your G*uns*"
> "Why Are We Choosing between Lives and G*uns*?"
> "If Nobody had a *Gun*, Nobody would Need a *Gun!*"
> "Protect Kids, Not *Guns*"
> "When Will We Love Our Kids More than Our *Guns*?"
> "My Right to Safety > Your Right to a *Gun*"

Got that? It's the *guns* that done it!

Time for a reality check.

Would eliminating guns eliminate violence? Of course not.

We never hear about *knife violence* or *vehicle violence* or *explosives violence*. Why? Probably because most normal people would immediately see the absurdity of it.

Most people own kitchen knives and automobiles, and they know that it's the person holding the knife, or driving the car, or setting off the explosives that makes the item dangerous to other human beings. There were no cries to ban Ryder trucks after the April 2018 Toronto van attack that killed ten people. No talk of ending *van violence*. Not even the French proposed banning trucks after the cargo truck attack in Nice in July 2016, which left an astounding 86 dead and 548 injured.

The Heritage Foundation compiled an impressive list demonstrating that many of the worst mass killings in the United States did not involve firearms.[189] Here are only a few examples of mass killings not involving firearms:[190]

- In 2017, a man rented a truck and plowed down pedestrians on a Manhattan bike path killing eight people and injuring eleven.[191]
- In 1995, a man parked a truck bomb outside the Alfred P. Murrah Federal Building in Oklahoma City, Oklahoma, killing 168 people and injuring more than six hundred.[192]
- In 1990, an angry ex-lover burned down the Happy Land social club killing eighty-seven people.[193]
- In 1987, a disgruntled former airline employee hijacked and crashed a passenger plane killing forty-three people.[194]
- In 1973, an arsonist killed thirty-two and injured fifteen at the Upstairs Lounge in New Orleans.[195]

And, to appeal to globalism for Justice Ruth Bader Ginsberg's benefit, we can look overseas to Germany where in 2015, a commercial airline pilot intentionally crashed a jetliner murdering 150 people.[196]

Reviewing ancient history reaffirms the obvious point that guns don't kill; criminals and violent people kill. The Greeks and the Romans lacked firearms, but did a great job discovering ways to violently kill one another. Cain did a number on Abel before the invention of firearms. And I don't recall seeing any firearms (if you don't count the dragons) in *Game of Thrones*. Yet there is no shortage or lack of mortal violence and criminality in that series.

Is there something special or magnetic about guns themselves that increase crimes or is it just media bias?

If the level of gun ownership were a good predictor of violence, then the United States—which leads the world in gun ownership by a wide margin—should top the world in violence statistics. In fact, according to the World Economic Forum (that's the same group that brings us Davos every year) the United States is not even in the top fifty most violent nations; and we came in just behind the United Kingdom, Italy, France, and Germany in safety rankings, among other countries.[197] Only four American cities (St. Louis, Baltimore, New Orleans, and Detroit) made the list of the worlds' fifty most violent cities.[198]

Somehow, the rate of violence in the United States is about the same as that of Western industrialized nations that are essentially gun-free. How can that be?

In the real world, people commit violence in all sorts of ways. They use guns, yes, but they also use knives, bats, pipes, vehicles, sledgehammers, and explosives.

People even use their fists and feet. According to the FBI's crime statistics, just over 15,000 homicides were committed in the United States in 2016. Of those, 374 were committed using a rifle and 262 with a shotgun—but 1,604 were committed using a knife, 1,798 by a weapon other than a gun or knife, and 656 using hands or feet.[199]

If instruments other than guns are used in violent attacks, why do media single out and label certain crimes "gun violence"?

Ye olde and charming London, England, offers perhaps the best demonstration of the truth that violence doesn't disappear when guns do. The city is a gun controller's paradise: The United Kingdom has some of the tightest gun restrictions in the world, including a ban on handguns. But in early 2018, London's murder rate surpassed New York City's.[200] It turns out that knifings have become an epidemic in London. London has grown so dangerous that Great Britain is now discussing whether to issue guns to its police.[201]

In June 2017, three terrorists used a van to run over pedestrians on the London Bridge before then stabbing people in a local marketplace.[202] The result: eight killed and forty-eight injured, including four unarmed police officers.[203] The bad guys were finally stopped when shot dead by *armed* police.[204] Apparently, you should not bring a billy club to a knife fight.

Britain is not the only place where criminals have turned to knives. In China, a group of knife-wielding thugs killed twenty-nine people and injured another 130 at a train station in a single attack.[205] Earlier this year, a twenty-eight-year-old man, who had been bullied at his former school, returned and killed nine middle school students and injured twelve more—all with a *knife*.[206]

The absurdity of the gun grabbers' position is further shown if we rewrite their protest signs to apply to other types of violence not involving guns. How would you react to the following?

"End Van Violence"
"My Right to Safety > Your Right to a Truck"
"Our Lives Are Worth More than Your Right to Rent a Truck"
"Down with Ford and Chevy"
"Protect Kids, Not Priuses"
"Lives before Knives"
"Tell the Food Network to Stop Idolizing Knives"
"Our Lives Are Worth More than Your Knives"
"Nobody Needs to Own a Professional Chef's Knife"

When signs like these mention the magic word "guns," the signs grace the covers of major U.S. papers beside headlines proclaiming things like "a new era of gun control is near" and "teenagers are leading the country to the promised land" and so on. But if you substitute any other object for "guns," the best publicity such signs could hope to garner would be on the cover of *The Onion*.

Do the promoters of the term *gun violence* have a hidden agenda? You be the judge. The focus should be on the criminal, not on the tool he uses.

The gun grabbers say: "Guns kill 96 Americans each day."

The truth: Guns are inanimate objects. Two-thirds of the people who die from gunshots each day commit suicide.

It's only my opinion, but the gun grabbers lie. There is no simpler way to put it. You can call it manipulating data, using selective language, or making false comparisons. At the end of the day, I submit that it's all a bunch of lies.

You think this is the fake news? Well, here are the facts.

Let's look at a line David Hogg loves to use. The line comes from his de facto leader, Michael Bloomberg, who founded and funds the anti-gun group Everytown for Gun Safety. Right on its website, the group says, "Every day, 96 Americans are killed with guns." [207]

This language creates the impression that ninety-six people are murdered every day with a gun.[208] This is false. Two-thirds of the people in that statistic committed suicide. Only about thirty a day are killed by another person using a gun. Meanwhile, 101 die each day in the United States in motor vehicle accidents. Among those, more than four each day are children under fifteen.[209] In comparison, approximately 3.5 kids under eighteen die each day as a victim of a gun homicide.[210]

Now, we all would say that thirty is still a lot of lives, and we all wish the number were smaller. But why mislead people about the real number and pretend that they're innocents on the way to the public library? When someone overdoses, we don't say they were killed by pills or protest in front of the local pharmacy.

Lumping suicides and homicides together is especially misleading because, as we'll see in a later chapter, there is no evidence to show that restricting people's access to guns lowers the suicide rate. Plenty of countries with strict gun control laws have higher suicide rates than the United States.

And isn't it also a bit weird that the same liberals who support right-to-die laws suddenly start objecting to suicide if you choose to end your life with a gun. What's with that? Why are they objecting if you happen to use a gun? Are they upset that you didn't get a doctor's prescription? Is that covered under Obamacare? Or are they just pretending to care about one's "right to choose" to die because it helps them make guns look bad?

And it's not just the anti-gun lobby and the coastal elites who want to distort the facts. It's our own government too. The Centers for Disease Control

(CDC) pulls the same magic trick by inventing "gun violence" death statistics. The CDC combines murders and suicides into one number that they call "Firearm Deaths,"[211] and then they publicize that number to the press every year, so the media can run stories that create a false impression that "gun crime" is far more prevalent in the United States than it really is.

But what happens if we look at the real numbers and ignore the distortions, which essentially compare apples to oranges.

If you ignore the meaningless and contrived "Firearm Deaths" rate and look at the CDC's murder "Homicide Mortality" rates, then we find gun-friendly states are far safer than gun control states.[212] In fact, many gun-friendly American states such as Vermont, New Hampshire, Maine, and North Dakota have homicide rates that compare very favorably to countries the gun grabbers idolize as models of safety, such as Canada, Belgium, the United Kingdom, and Australia.[213]

By focusing only on deaths involving firearms, including suicides, the gun grabbers create a false impression that more guns lead to more violence.

But I ask a simple question: Would you feel safer walking down the streets of the gun grabbers' dream city, Chicago (762 murders in 2016),[214] or the mean streets of gun-friendly Vermont (ten murders in 2016),[215] where every law-abiding adult can carry a concealed handgun without a license?

The gun grabbers say: "Guns make society less safe."

The truth: More guns mean *more* safety.

Anti-gunners argue that the presence of a gun increases the likelihood of murder and mayhem.

This is obviously untrue.

States such as Vermont, North Dakota, New Hampshire, Wyoming, and Idaho that have some of the highest rates of gun ownership in the country also have some of the lowest murder rates, according to the CDC's data.[216] Conversely, tough gun control states like Maryland and Illinois have some of the highest murder rates.[217]

The most dangerous parts of the United States are those that actively work to restrict gun ownership.[218] There is a wide disparity between counties with high murders and those with few or none. As of 2014, the worst 1 percent of counties accounted for 37 percent of all murders; the worst 2 percent accounted for 51 percent of all murders; and the worst 5 percent accounted for 68 percent.[219] Meanwhile, 69 percent of U.S. counties had no murders or only one for all of 2014.[220]

Even within counties, murder rates vary dramatically by neighborhood. Most of Chicago's murders occurred in just twelve of the city's seventy-seven neighborhoods.[221] In Washington, D.C., almost all the murders occurred in the part of the city east of 14th Street NW.[222]

There are very large sections of the country with high gun ownership rates and zero murders.[223]

Similarly, a 2015 study by the Crime Prevention Research Center showed that murder rates have fallen about 25 percent since 2007—even as the number of concealed-carry handgun permits nearly tripled during the same period."[224]

The gun grabbers say: "The United States should be more like other civilized countries that ban or limit private gun ownership."

The truth: The United States has far lower crimes rates than virtually every country in the Western Hemisphere including all of those that ban or severely limit private gun ownership.

Comparing the United States only to European countries is racist, right? Aren't the gun grabbers acting like a group of Eurocentric, post-colonialist racists? Well, we don't want to emulate that, do we?

Let's skip those Euro-comparisons and look closer to home for comparisons; specifically, let's look south to Latin America. Virtually all Latin American countries are anti-gun and make it hard for any ordinary person to get a firearm.

And how do the violence rates in the "dangerous" gun-friendly United States compare to the anti-gun Western Hemisphere countries, many of which supply the U.S. with scores of Dreamers and other "new Americans,"[225] and others to which Americans flock as vacation destinations? Let's go to the scoreboard to see how pro-gun control countries fare in the murder column. These numbers come from the United Nations Office of Drugs and Crime (UNODC) and show murder rates per 100,000 inhabitants using the most recent numbers available:

4. U.S. Virgin Islands—49.3
5. Jamaica—47.0
7. Belize—37.6
9. St. Kitts and Nevis—34.2
12. Brazil—29.5
13. Bahamas—28.4
21. Mexico—19.3
24. Puerto Rico—18.5
29. Dominican Republic—15.2
34. Bermuda—13.0
36. Costa Rica—11.9
42. Barbados—10.9
44. Antigua and Barbuda—10.3
59. British Virgin Islands—8.4
87. Argentina—5.9
90. United States—5.4[226]

The gun grabbers will be surprised to learn that the United States is much safer than those countries to our south, virtually all of which embrace radical forms of gun control.

The gun grabbers say: **"The mainstream media engages in honest and fair reporting of gun issues."**

The truth: The mainstream media, based largely in liberal bastion cities of New York, Los Angeles, and Washington, D.C., is biased against firearms and gun rights.

But you won't hear any of this from the mainstream media. The media's anti-gun bias is obvious.

In the summer of 2017, *Politico* crunched data about the "media bubble" and concluded, "The media bubble is worse than you think."[227] *Politico* noted: "Resist—if you can—the conservative reflex to absorb this data and conclude that the media deliberately twists the news in favor of Democrats. Instead, take it the way a social scientist would take it: The people who report, edit, produce and publish news can't help being affected—deeply affected—by the environment around them."[228]

Former *New York Times* public editor Daniel Okrent touched on the same point in a 2004 column that merits rereading today. "The 'heart, mind, and habits' of the *Times*," he wrote, "cannot be divorced from the ethos of the cosmopolitan city where it is produced. On such subjects as abortion, gay rights, gun control, and environmental regulation, the *Times'* news reporting is a pretty good reflection of its region's dominant predisposition. And yes, a *Times*-ian ethos flourishes in all of internet publishing's major cities—Los Angeles, New York, Boston, Seattle, San Francisco and Washington. The *Times* thinks of itself as a centrist national newspaper, but it's more accurate to say its politics are perfectly centered on the slices of America that look and think the most like Manhattan."[229]

The media's bias against guns has consequences. As economist John Lott said, "If Americans hear only about the bad things that happen with guns, they will be much more likely to support strict gun regulations. The unjustified fears may also disarm people and prevent them from saving lives."[230]

The media's anti-gun bias could be seen in the post-Parkland "news coverage." Even the Bloomberg-funded website *The Trace* admitted that the news coverage after the Parkland shooting was far greater than any other high-profile shooting including the Southland, Texas, shooting where a good guy with an AR-15 stopped the attack.[231]

Bias helps explain why the national media only rarely discuss the defensive use of guns. Tellingly, the one "defensive action" story they did cover involved an African American man who used his bare hands to disarm a gunman who opened fire at a Waffle House in Tennessee killing four people.[232]

In a strange contrast, that same week another crazy person tried to kill someone in another Waffle House—only to be shot by a good guy with a gun.[233] While the national media went crazy covering the first story, about someone stopping a gunman without a gun,[234] the media went silent about the second story of a man with a gun stopping a murder.

Coincidence? Not a chance.

Chapter 6
Gun Grabber Myth #4
"We Need to Ban Assault Weapons"

But Let's Start with Assault Trucks, Assault Rope, Assault Hands and Feet, and Assault Knives

The gun grabbers say: "Nobody wants to ban guns (wink, wink)—we just want to ban 'assault weapons.'"

The truth: No ordinary American *has* an "assault weapon."

No matter what you hear from the media, politicians, and gun grabbers, ordinary American citizens don't have "assault weapons." What some citizens own are semiautomatic rifles, which look like military rifles but have very different capabilities.

With a semiautomatic firearm, whether a rifle or an ordinary handgun, you must pull the gun's trigger each time you fire a bullet. By contrast, with a fully automatic gun (always a rifle), you can pull and hold the trigger and the gun will fire multiple bullets until you release the trigger or run out of bullets. The military uses fully automatic firearms.

The gun most often labeled an "assault weapon" is probably the AR-15, the most popular rifle in America today.[235] The AR-15 is nothing more than an ordinary civilian rifle that happens to be painted black; it is much less deadly than other guns, including many wood-stock deer rifles. Many people think that the "AR" in the name is short for "assault rifle," but it's not. The letters stand for "ArmaLite Rifle," ArmaLite being the company that originally developed it.

The military doesn't use AR-15s. That firearm is not an "assault rifle." Again, it's a semiautomatic firearm.

Despite the attention focused on it today, the AR-15 is not some new phenomenon. It has been in commercial production since *Leave It to Beaver* was airing new episodes more than a half-century ago.[236]

AR-15s are the most popular rifle in America today for good reason. They are easier to control than handguns, highly accurate, reliable, fun to shoot, and serve as an invaluable self-defense tool. They also offer the advantage of thirty rounds of protection. The AR-15s' low recoil makes them a great gun for women to shoot. And if used with the proper ammunition, bullets fired with an AR-15 are less likely to penetrate a wall, which makes them safer than most handguns by reducing the risk of inadvertently shooting a neighbor or family member in an adjacent room.

Ask the people of Sutherland Springs, Texas. In November 2017, a gun-wielding lunatic entered the town's First Baptist Church on a Sunday morning and opened fire, killing twenty-six people and wounding twenty. A nearby resident, Stephen Willeford, heard the shots, grabbed his AR-15, and chased the shooter. The two exchanged gunfire. During the high-speed chase that followed, the mass murderer crashed his car, then shot himself. "If it wasn't for [Willeford], the guy wouldn't have stopped," one witness said.[237]

That's not the first time an AR-15 has been used to save lives. Take a look at this list from the Heritage Foundation:

- Oswego, Illinois (2018): Dave Thomas used an AR-15 to prevent his neighbor from being harmed (or killed) by an aggressor with a knife.[238]
- Catawba County, North Carolina (2018): A seventeen-year-old and his AR-15 successfully fought off three armed attackers.[239]
- Houston, Texas (2017): A homeowner survived a drive-by shooting by defending himself with his AR-15.[240]

- Broken Arrow, Oklahoma (2017): Zach Peters, living in his parents' home, killed three would-be burglars with an AR-15.[241]
- Ferguson, Missouri (2014): Derrick Jordan, armed with an AR-15, and two friends, protected a store owner from rioters.[242]
- Harris County, Texas (2013): A 15-year-old boy armed with an AR-15 saved his life and that of his 12-year-old sister during a home invasion.[243]
- Rochester, New York (2013): A college student scared off home intruders with an AR-15.[244]

No one needs an AR-15? I'm sure these folks and the people of Sutherland Springs would have a few things to say about the benefits of these so-called assault rifles.

So sure, ordinary Americans don't need "assault rifles."

Until they do.

Just like ordinary Americans don't need seat belts.

Until they do.

Evil people will always find a way to do evil things. We protect our children and ourselves with our firearms. Giving a gun a scary name like "assault rifle" may be an effective rhetorical device but is total nonsense.

Interestingly, the federal government has acknowledged this. When the United States Department of Homeland Security buys variants of the

AR-15—but with fully automatic capabilities—it doesn't call them "assault weapons"; it describes them as firearms "suitable for personal defense."[245]

If gun grabbers really want to keep Americans safe, why do they focus so much attention on "assault rifles"? Did you know that rifles *of any kind* were used in only 2.5 percent of all murders committed in the United States in 2016?[246] That's according to the FBI's official crime statistics.[247]

Why aren't gun grabbers campaigning to ban knives, clubs, and even hands and feet—all of which claim far more lives than rifles do? Knives, for example, were used in nearly five times as many murders in 2016 as rifles.[248]

Handguns were used in nine times as many murders as were rifles, shotguns, and other guns *combined* in 2016, according to the Uniform Crime Reporting data,[249] and the FBI's 2016 crime data show handguns were used in *nineteen times* as many murders as rifles.

When it comes to "mass shootings," a Rockefeller Institute of Government study found that the preferred weapon of mass shooters was not a so-called "assault rifle," but was actually a handgun. Handguns were chosen by mass shooters over "assault weapons" by a 3 to 1 margin.[250]

If gun grabbers really want to save lives, wouldn't they be better off trying to ban handguns than AR-15s?

Then again, let's not give 'em any ideas...

★ ★ ★

The gun grabbers say: "The Founding Fathers did not envision modern firearms, so the Second Amendment doesn't protect these dangerous weapons."

The truth: The Founders understood that firearms technology was rapidly advancing, and high-capacity magazines had already been invented years *before* the Second Amendment was written.

★ ★ ★

The gun grabbers, including some judges, say that the Founders never envisioned assault rifles with high-capacity magazines, so these firearms should not be protected under the Second Amendment.[251]

So what?

The Founders didn't envision a lot of things. Living in an age of pamphleteers, they did not foresee the telegraph or the telephone, to say nothing of the internet, cable TV, and the iPhone. Does that mean we should turn our backs on the First Amendment?

Or should we throw the Fourth Amendment away because it talks about people being secure in their papers but doesn't say diddly about email?

Too many hucksters want us to believe that the Constitution is about "things" when it's not. The Constitution is about our freedoms as American citizens.

The Constitution makes no distinction between one firearm and another. If the Constitution started making distinctions among things, then it would start distinguishing among the internet, TV, and newspapers. But the First Amendment applies to all media equally.

In any case, it's misleading to say that the Framers of the Constitution did not envision more sophisticated firearms. They may not have imagined modern rifles specifically, but the Girandoni air rifle, which had a twenty-round magazine, was invented a decade *before* the Bill of Rights was written.[252] Various multi-shot and multi-barreled guns already existed as well, even if they were not widely deployed because of cost and complexity (sort of like Tesla cars today).[253]

The Founders were intimately involved in the production of armaments during the American Revolution because they had to be. They knew how far firearm technology had come since the days of matchlocks in the fifteenth century. They also were farsighted enough to give Eli Whitney (inventor of the cotton gin) a contract for muskets using the new technology of interchangeable parts.[254]

More broadly, the Founders recognized constant improvements occurring in all areas of invention. Some of the Founders were innovators themselves.

Benjamin Franklin was famous for his inventions: the lightning rod, bifocal glasses, and the Franklin stove.[255]

Thomas Jefferson was famous too: for the swivel chair, the hideaway bed, the pedometer, and the dumbwaiter.[256]

George Washington developed several farming innovations at Mount Vernon.[257]

Understanding the importance of technology improvement, the Framers provided for a patent system right in the Constitution. Article I, Section 8, Clause 8 says that Congress shall have the power "to promote the progress of science and useful arts, by securing for limited times to authors and inventors the exclusive right to their respective writings and discoveries."

Why include this in Article 1 if they anticipated living in a static world?

The gun grabbers say: "We need to eliminate high-capacity magazines."

The truth: A ban on high-capacity magazines will not deter determined killers.

Anti-gunners like to pass laws that let them say, "We did something." But these laws don't deter bad guys from crime; they hurt only the law-abiding.

Take laws limiting the capacity of gun magazines.[258] Eight states and the District of Columbia have imposed such restrictions.[259] Usually magazines are limited to ten rounds, but a couple of states set the maximum capacity at fifteen rounds.[260] Do these restrictions limit crime? Hardly. From 1994 to 2004, the federal Assault Weapons Ban limited magazines that held more than ten rounds.[261] During that ten-year period, the gun-related murder rate was 19.3 percent higher than after the ban expired.[262]

But do the limits stop mass shootings? No.

Consider the 2018 Parkland school shootings. The March for Our Lives movement that emerged after the shootings set as one of its main objectives to institute a "high-capacity magazine ban."[263] But the Parkland shooter *did not use* high-capacity magazines. He used only ten-round magazines in his rifle.[264]

Or look at the Sante Fe, Texas, shooting in May 2018. The killer used a shotgun (likely holding between 5 and 10 rounds of ammunition) and a revolver (holding no more than six rounds of ammunition) to kill ten people.[265]

What about the 2007 Virginia Tech shootings? The perpetrator didn't even use a rifle; he used two semiautomatic pistols—a .22 caliber and a 9 mm. He had as many as nineteen magazines holding ten to fifteen rounds each.[266]

Limiting magazine size to ten rounds would have had little to no impact on the lethality of these attacks.

Of course, it's easy to imagine gun grabbers using this fact to argue for even *stricter* limits on magazines down the road. Sure, a ten-round limit is the standard now. But maybe it will be seven rounds next year. And maybe two rounds or even one round after that. Here we see the slippery slope of gun control arguments. Gun grabbers take an incremental approach to their ultimate goal of total gun confiscation.

Anyone who insists that magazine capacity limits will deter a madman bent on committing mass murder is naive or else has an entirely different agenda. A determined killer will find a way to kill. Look at the 2016 attack in Nice, France, in which a terrorist drove a nineteen-ton truck into a crowd, killing eighty-six people.[267] Or look at the 2018 Toronto, Canada, attack in which the killer drove a van into a crowd, killing ten.[268]

Limiting Americans' access to high-capacity magazines merely limits Americans' right to self-defense. It endangers the innocent and the law-abiding, giving proactive criminals an even greater advantage. Remember, criminals by definition disobey the law. When high-capacity magazines are outlawed, only outlaws (and the government) will have high-capacity magazines.

Why should civilians have high-capacity magazines? One would be hard-pressed to find anyone who has ever been in a shootout saying he wished he had brought less ammunition. Crime is often a group activity. Columbine had two shooters.[269] San Bernardino had two shooters.[270] September 11 involved nineteen attackers.[271] The Bataclan theater shooting in Paris had at least seven attackers.[272] Crime gangs all have multiple members. And the list goes on.

Even if you are facing one criminal, a single shot or even multiple rounds can be insufficient to win the battle. You might miss with several rounds. Or you might confront a criminal high on drugs like PCP or meth who can be shot multiple times without going down.

Simply put: You need high-capacity magazines because there are high-capacity criminals. More ammunition is always better. Once you're out of ammo, you're out of the fight—and perhaps possibly dead.

There's a reason police carry extra loaded magazines on their duty belt and/or in their cruisers: their lives depend on it. But states like New York, New Jersey, Vermont, and California have decided that the police get the benefit of being protected by high-capacity magazines while ordinary peons, including family members of the police, are denied the right and ability to protect themselves from the same criminal predators.

Law-abiding Americans are safer in their homes when they can defend themselves against criminals. If a criminal has a firearm with a seventeen-round magazine or multiple guns each with ten rounds, then the person trying to keep his or her home and family safe should be able to have a firearm with seventeen or more rounds as well.

A homeowner faced with an intruder would be even safer with a thirty-round magazine.

Chapter 7
Gun Grabber Myth #5
"Gun-Free Zones Are Nirvana"

*Gun-Free Zones Are Catnip for
Criminals*

The gun grabbers say: "Gun-free zones prevent mass
shootings."

**The truth: Gun-free zones create a magnet for bad
people who want to hurt good people.**

Forget what the politicians say, gun-free zones are
very dangerous.

Politicians create "gun-free zones," pat themselves
on the back for their foresight, hang "gun-free zone"
signs with those threatening red circles and the line
through the middle and think that they have solved some
problem.

They haven't.

In fact, they have probably made the perceived
problem more dangerous.

In their desire to "do something," politicians and do-gooders carve out easy "kill zones" for violent psychopaths. There is a reason mass shootings don't happen at police stations or at gun ranges: there are no sitting ducks in places where everyone is armed.

Did you know that just about every mass shooting has occurred in a gun-free zone? A comprehensive study done by the Crime Prevention Research Center found that more than 97 percent of the mass shootings since 1950 occurred in gun-free zones where civilians are not permitted to carry firearms.[273]

Are we supposed to believe it's a coincidence that mass shootings virtually always occur in places where those "come and get us" gun-free-zone signs are posted?

Don't the gun grabbers understand that when a terrorist or a mentally-troubled youth sees a gun-free-zone sign, he reads it instead as saying "Unarmed People Here" or "Easy Targets Here"? Gun-free zones are a magnet for aspiring mass shooters.

Most people know that places like schools and other government buildings are generally gun-free zones. Some of the highest-profile mass shootings have occurred at gun-free schools, including Parkland (seventeen killed)[274], Oregon Community College (nine killed)[275], Newtown (twenty-seven killed)[276], Virginia Tech (thirty-two killed)[277], and Columbine (thirteen killed).[278] Shootings have also occurred at gun-free government facilities like San Bernardino (fourteen killed)[279] and twice at Fort Hood, in 2009 (thirteen killed)[280] and 2014 (three killed).[281]

What is less known is that many of the private or nongovernment locations where mass shootings have occurred prohibited carrying guns. Some recent examples include:

- In 2018, a shooter took aim at a Waffle House in Antioch, Tennessee.[282] The Waffle House was designated as a gun-free zone.[283] Result: four killed.[284]

- In 2017, a recently fired employee entered through the back door of his former workplace in Orlando, Florida.[285] The business was not open to the public and had a no-gun rule for the employees.[286] Result: five killed.[287]

- In 2016, a gunman entered the Cascade Mall in Burlington, Washington.[288] The mall has a code of conduct that prohibits all weapons, including concealed-carry firearms.[289] Result: five killed.[290]

- In 2015, a shooter opened fire on the Emanuel African Methodist Episcopal Church in Charleston, South Carolina.[291] State law prohibits the carrying of guns in places of worship unless express permission is obtained from the church.[292] Result: nine killed.[293]

- In 2012, a man opened fire at his workplace in Minneapolis, Minnesota, hours after losing his job.[294] The business had a no-firearms policy.[295] Result: six killed.[296]
- In 2012, a man shot up a Cinemark Theater in Aurora, Colorado.[297] The state allows businesses to determine their own gun policy and the theater was a gun-free zone.[298] Result: twelve killed.[299]

Again, it is no coincidence that these mass shooters chose gun-free spaces to attack. In some cases, such as when a fired employee shot up his former workplace, you can speculate that he happened to work in a gun-free zone and that this policy had nothing to do with his actions. But when you look at the overall numbers, it makes more sense to conclude that criminals, even in a moment of insanity, calculate a lesser risk in a place where guns are prohibited and a greater likelihood that they will be able to carry out their evil plans.

Of course, if you listen to the gun controllers, this isn't about gun-free zones at all; it's about America and our love of guns. Mass shootings don't happen in the rest of the world, they tell us; we need to get rid of our guns as all the civilized people have already done.

Well, the facts tell a different story. The Crime Prevention Research Center points out that more casualties, both deaths and injuries, resulted from mass shootings in mostly gun-free France in one year (2015) than in the United States during the entire eight years of

President Obama's presidency.[300] Keep in mind that the United States has five times the population of France.

Looking more closely at France, Erich Pratt, executive director of the Gun Owners of America, notes: "France has far more gun control than we do. The French have greater restrictions on semi-automatic 'assault weapons,' which are falsely labeled as such by newspapers like *USA Today*. Yet gun ownership restrictions in France did not stop terrorists from murdering 130 people at a concert in 2015."[301]

In a direct comparison between the United States and the nations of Europe, the U.S. didn't even make the top ten in the rate of frequency of mass shootings.[302] Macedonia led the way at a rate of .471 per million; others ahead of the United States included Switzerland, Norway, Finland, Belgium, Austria, the Czech Republic, and France.[303] The United States landed at #12.[304]

The gun grabbers say: "We need to ban guns to keep them out of the hands of criminals."

The truth: Criminals always find ways to get guns and other weapons.

There is a well-known adage: "When guns are outlawed, only outlaws will have guns."

That's true. Banning guns won't prevent criminals from getting guns.

First, common sense tells us this is true. By some estimates, nearly 80 percent of gun-related crimes are carried out with illegally-owned firearms (like the school shootings in Santa Fe, Texas, and Parkland, Florida).[305] What should make us think that laws against guns will stop criminals from getting guns? Criminals, by definition, purposefully disobey laws. They don't abide by the rules of civilized society and don't care what the laws say. Guns are one of the tools of their "trade," and they will always be able to get the tools they need. Always.

Think of it this way: murder and robbery are against the law, but that doesn't mean we have eliminated murder and robbery.

We don't have to rely on common sense to see that gun bans are unwise. Gun bans have been tried before—and they haven't worked.

Virtually all of Western Europe has banned or severely restricted private gun ownership.[306] Yet in the 2015 attack on the Amsterdam–Paris train (portrayed in the 2018 movie *The 15:17 to Paris*), the assailant somehow got his hands on an AK-47 and a Luger pistol.[307] In the coordinated series of attacks that took 130 lives in Paris in 2015, the criminals had fully automatic weapons.[308]

Mexico has but a single gun store because private guns are mostly banned there.[309] Yet somehow the Mexican crime cartels seem to be armed to the teeth as they kill government officials, judges, and tourists almost daily. Tellingly, the Mexican cartels have started to make their own guns and weapons, which further illustrates how criminals will always find a way to get guns (regardless of what the law says).[310]

And remember, criminals can kill lots and lots of people using weapons like knives, acid, trucks, and explosives.

Australia has almost no guns but experiences plenty of violent crime. Australia's armed and unarmed robbery rates increased significantly in the five years following the passage of its National Firearms Act.[311] You'd never guess that, however, if you listen only to the gun controllers and the praise they heap on Australia.

We see multi-casualty knife attacks in China, France, and London.[312] We see the Boston Marathon and Chelsea bombers using pressure-cooker bombs.[313] We see criminals driving vans into crowds of people in Nice, France, and Toronto, Canada.[314] We even see Palestinians flying "incendiary kites" to cause major fire damage to Israel.[315]

Or ask Sweden how things are working out with hand grenades. Sweden has restrictive gun regulations and in recent years has seen a huge upswing in grenade attacks. Grenades left from the Bosnian War have made their way to Sweden and into the hands of gangs and organized crime.[316] *The New York Times* recently reported that "[i]llegal weapons often enter Sweden" over a bridge that connects the country to Denmark—a bridge that formerly "symbolized the unfurling of a vibrant, borderless Europe," but now "has been more closely associated with smuggling of people, weapons and drugs," according to the *Times*.[317]

It is pure fantasy to think that banning guns will make Americans safer; it will accomplish the reverse.

Gun bans deprive law-abiding citizens of the ability to defend themselves. So, they create a new class of readily identifiable potential victims. Women, the elderly, the sick, and smaller men all become obvious prey. The ban emboldens violent criminals.

Look at what has happened in Brazil. The country has extremely restrictive gun laws, including a ban on carrying firearms in public, a mandatory firearms registry, a minimum age requirement of twenty-five, and expensive and onerous licensing requirements.[318]

Brazil deals with about forty thousand gun murders every year.[319] Even NPR has noted the frightening developments in Brazil: "Almost 60,000 people were murdered in Brazil in 2014, most with guns. While some Latin American countries have higher per capita murder rates, in absolute numbers, Brazil is the deadliest place in the world outside Syria. Brazilians are far more likely to be shot to death than Americans, a more populous country where there are about 8,000 to 9,000 gun homicides each year."[320]

Brazil instituted strict gun control laws, and the results have been terrifying. Is it any wonder that support for gun ownership is gaining ground there? As *Bloomberg* put it in a headline, "People Are Ready to Buy Some Guns in the World's Murder Capital."[321]

The lesson here is clear: Once you give up your right to effective self-defense, the criminals get you bad.

The gun grabbers say: "Mass public shootings have become an epidemic; we're much less safe than we used to be."

The truth: We're much *safer* than we were twenty years ago because the country has more guns, more gun owners, and more people conceal-carry handguns.

Here are the facts: as the number of guns has increased in this country, the number of gun deaths has declined dramatically.

Although it is difficult to give precise numbers on gun ownership, a report by the Congressional Research Service estimated that overall civilian firearms in the United States increased from approximately 192 million in 1994 to 310 million in 2009.[322] Since that time, gun ownership has increased exponentially.

A 2017 ATF report on firearms commerce showed a "43 percent increase in firearms manufacturing in the U.S." from 2011–2015.[323] "In 2015, the number of firearms manufactured grew to more than 9.3 million, up from the approximate 6.5 million firearms manufactured in 2011."[324]

The National Instant Criminal Background Check System (NICS) is a strong indication of new gun sales in the United States. During the Obama era, it was not unusual to see month after month of record NICS background checks being performed.[325]

The number of nationwide concealed carry permits also increased significantly during the latter part of the Obama administration and continues to grow today with women comprising 36 percent of permit holders in the fourteen states that provide data by gender in 2016.[326] In July 2017, the Crime Prevention Research Center estimated that there were over 16.3 million concealed carry permit holders in the United States, which means approximately 6.5 percent of adults nationwide have a concealed handgun permit.[327] But even that estimate is too low because it doesn't account for gun owners in states like New York where concealed carry data is not available or in the fourteen states that have constitutional carry, which means that a permit is not required to conceal carry.[328]

Yet gun deaths have declined significantly. That same Congressional Research Service report stated that the number of firearms-related murder victims dropped from 17,073 in 1993 to 10,031 in 2009.[329] Since the U.S. population increased so much during that period, the *rate* of firearm-related murders was cut in half.

Similarly, the U.S. Department of Justice reported: "Firearm-related homicides dropped from 18,253 homicides in 1993 to 11,101 in 2011, and nonfatal firearm crimes dropped from 1.5 million victimizations in 1993 to 467,300 in 2011."[330]

Yes, it's true: We're safer today than we were twenty years ago (the exception being for those living in gun-free zones).

But this raises a crucial question: Why does it seem to so many people that life is getting less safe?

The answer is largely because of the horrifying mass public shootings over the past two decades. But the prominence of these incidents skews our perception. Mass killings account for only 0.2 percent of homicides every year; only 12 percent of mass killings are mass public shootings (not involving family member, felony robberies, or gang violence).[331] These rare events are, understandably, the subject of wall-to-wall media coverage.

Psychologists have a fancy term for this skewing effect: the "availability heuristic." As one psychological study puts it, "the easier it is for people to call to mind examples of a phenomenon, the more frequently they think it happens."[332]

With that in mind, think about the psychological effects of television news. Writing in *Psychology Today*, Dr. Graham Davey says that because of the need to fill twenty-four hours a day with content, "there is also an increasing tendency for news broadcasters to 'emotionalize' their news and to do so by emphasizing any potential negative outcomes of a story no matter how low the risks of those negative outcomes might be." Dr.

Davey adds, "This is basically 'scaremongering' at every available opportunity to sensationalize and emotionalize the impact of a news story."[333]

It's the basic mantra of the news industry: *If it bleeds, it leads.* But now the news outlets don't just report on the bleeding; they emotionalize it.

In 2016, after the Orlando Pulse nightclub shooting, the Media Research Center analyzed forty-seven gun policy stories and ten other stories that mentioned gun policy on ABC's *World News Tonight*, the *CBS Evening News*, the *NBC Nightly News*, ABC's *Good Morning America*, *CBS This Morning*, and NBC's *Today*.[334] Statements on the network news programs favored gun control over gun rights by a ratio of eight to one. Gun control advocates received 65 minutes and 12 seconds of coverage.[335] Gun rights advocates received 8 minutes and 12 seconds.[336]

Northeastern University professor of criminology James Alan Fox studied mass school shootings—the incidents, like the Parkland shootings, that dominate news coverage and lead so many people to believe that school shootings have become an epidemic.[337] After crunching the numbers, Dr. Fox concluded that both the number of school shootings and the overall number of victims has *declined* since the 1990s.[338] He recently told NPR (not known for its support of right-leaning issues), "Schools are safer today than they had been in previous decades."[339]

So why don't people recognize this reality? "The difference is the impression, the perception that people have," Fox said.[340] "Today we have cell phone recordings of gunfire that play over and repeatedly. So, it's that the impression is very different. That's why people think things are a lot worse now, but the statistics say otherwise."[341]

USA Today got in on the act when it debunked the claims of the Michael Bloomberg-funded Everytown for Gun Safety. The paper pointed out: "Everytown for Gun Safety reported that there have been 290 school shootings since the catastrophic massacre in Newtown, Conn., more than five years ago. However, very few of these were anything akin to Sandy Hook or Parkland. Sure, they all involved a school of some type (including technical schools and colleges) as well as a firearm, but the outcomes were hardly similar. Nearly half of the 290 were completed or attempted suicides, accidental discharges of a gun, or shootings with not a single individual being injured. Of the remainder, the clear majority involved either one fatality or none at all."[342]

In March 2018, *New York* magazine (another outlet not known for being friendly to conservative views) ran a piece headlined bluntly: "There Is No 'Epidemic of Mass School Shootings.'"[343] The article explained:

> Spectacular acts of mass murder committed against children (especially upper-middle class children in "good" public schools) attract a degree of media

attention and political concern that our nation's (roughly) 20,000 annual firearm suicides—and daily acts of urban gang violence—simply do not. The most misleading piece of the Parkland survivors' message—that their experience is representative of a widespread social problem that threatens the lives of all American children—may well be its most politically effective component.[344]

That may be the most brutally honest statement ever made in a confirmed anti-gun publication. It's a blatant admission that the public is being emotionally manipulated, and that manipulation advances the gun grabbers' political agenda.

Chapter 8
Gun Grabber Myth #6
"It's Too Easy to Buy a Gun"

Actually, Guns Are Not Bad,
Accidents Are Rare, and Tons of
Gun Regulations Are Already on
the Books

The gun grabbers say: "It's too easy to get a gun. We need more regulations."

The truth: There are thousands of gun laws and regulations already on the books.

Gun grabbers complain that guns are too easy to get in America. They use lines like "There are more regulations on my car than on a gun" and "My uterus is more regulated than guns are."

This is nonsense. The only people who say it's too easy to get a gun are the people who have never gotten one. You must complete multiple pages of forms to undergo a background check. Some states have waiting periods. People who purchase firearms from reputable online merchants must travel to a nearby gun shop or other federal firearms licensee to take possession of their gun, at which point they must go through the same federal background check process.

The United States has thousands of gun laws and regulations on the books at the local, state, and federal levels.[345] These laws regulate all aspects of firearms: how you carry and store guns; the characteristics of guns you may buy and own; where you can shoot guns; what types of devices you can put on your gun (suppressors); the serial numbers on guns; gun store locations; the transportation of guns across state lines; who can own guns; who cannot own guns; who can sell guns—and the list goes on.

On the federal side, there are special licenses to manufacture, distribute, and sell guns. There are at least nine types of federal gun licenses that business owners need to secure, depending on which business they intend to perform:[346]

- Type 01—Dealer in Firearms Other Than Destructive Devices
- Type 02—Pawnbroker in Firearms Other Than Destructive Devices
- Type 03—Collector of Curios and Relics
- Type 06—Manufacturer of Ammunition for Firearms Other Than Ammunition for Destructive Devices or Armor Piercing Ammunition

- Type 07—Manufacturer of Firearms Other Than Destructive Devices
- Type 08—Importer of Firearms Other Than Destructive Devices or Ammunition for Firearms Other Than Destructive Devices, or Ammunition Other Than Armor Piercing Ammunition
- Type 09—Dealer in Destructive Devices
- Type 10—Manufacturer of Destructive Devices, Ammunition for Destructive Devices, or Armor Piercing Ammunition
- Type 11—Importer of Destructive Devices, Ammunition for Destructive Devices, or Armor Piercing Ammunition

On top of this, fifty different sets of state laws touch on firearms, including red flag laws allowing law enforcement and family members to petition a court to take away a person's guns in a dangerous situation, relinquishment laws requiring individuals to turn in their guns under certain situations, assault weapons bans, high-capacity magazine bans, gun possession prohibitions for high-risk individuals, gun possession prohibitions for individuals with domestic violence convictions or restraining orders, and mandatory background checks.

There are lawyers whose practice is devoted to advising companies and individuals on how to comply with the countless, confusing gun laws.

Even certain accessories are regulated to the hilt. Take suppressors, which are devices shaped like soup cans that, when attached to the barrel of a gun, muffle the intensity of the sound made with each shot the gun fires. Sports shooters and hunters use suppressors to prevent hearing loss from extremely loud gunshots.[347] But try to get a suppressor for your gun. You'd think somebody was asking for the combination to Fort Knox. Here's how one suppressor company[348] describes part of the process to its customers:

If you're buying as an individual, you will need to mail the following documents to the United States Department of Justice, Bureau of Alcohol, Tobacco & Firearms:

- Both copies of your completed Form 4s
- $200 check made payable to the Bureau of Alcohol, Tobacco, Firearms and Explosives
- Two passport-sized photos
- Two fingerprint cards
- Completed Form 5330.20

Two passport photos? Two sets of fingerprints? Multiple forms? A couple hundred dollars and a 3–6 month waiting period? You gotta be kidding me.

The gun grabbers say: "Anyone who intends to buy a gun should go through a background check."

The truth: We already *have* background checks.

Anytime someone uses a gun in a high-profile shooting, the gun grabbers call for universal background checks, no matter the circumstances of the incident. You'd think that anyone could just walk into a store and buy a gun like buying a gallon of milk. Hardly.

They talk about it so much you'd think that background checks were the panacea to solve the violence problem in this country. There's only one problem with that: we already have background checks that cover the vast majority of gun sales each year.

Mandatory background checks by gun retailers have been federal law since 1993.[349] To purchase a firearm from a federally licensed gun dealer (all commercial gun sellers must have a federal firearms license, or an FFL), the buyer must complete ATF Form 4473, which asks for all relevant personal information and requires the applicant to state whether he has ever been convicted of a felony or misdemeanor domestic violence, used illegal drugs, been a fugitive, or been committed to a mental institution.[350]

The only exceptions to the background check rule apply to people who already hold certain state gun licenses, such as a valid concealed carry permit (which requires a background check to qualify), and to gun transfers between private individuals. The gun grabbers focus a lot on the latter: private transactions involving, let's say, two neighbors in the same state (where neither is a licensed gun dealer) or two family members (including, say, a father giving a gift to his son). They refer to these ordinary transactions as the evil "gun show loophole."

Gun grabbers are obsessed with the so-called gun show loophole. They want to know about every single exchange between any two individuals anywhere in the country involving a gun. Only in the minds of liberals is it a crisis that every gun transaction is not carried out under the ever-watchful eye of Big Brother. Why? Well, that's easy.

The ultimate goal of the gun grabber is gun confiscation. But the government can't confiscate your guns if it doesn't know where they are hiding. A federal gun registry seems like the ideal solution, but the federal government is prohibited from creating such a registry under the 1993 background check law.[351] In states where gun registration laws have been enacted, as in New York with the Safe Act, the level of noncompliance is high.[352] The same situation exists in even more liberal Connecticut, where, despite serious penalties, people simply do not comply.[353]

So how do these liberals get around federal restrictions and ensure compliance by the locals? They want a nationwide searchable database of all gun sale records, which is just a backdoor way of creating a gun registry. If the government can search for the names of everyone who bought an AR-15 last year, then it essentially has a nationwide gun registry. And once the gun grabbers know who has the guns, then they know where to send the police to confiscate them; just like the Nazis did in 1930s Germany[354] and New York City did with gun bans.[355]

It shouldn't surprise you that the top two items on the March for Our Lives mission statement are universal background checks and a searchable database for the Bureau of Alcohol, Tobacco, and Firearms (ATF).[356]

If you think gun confiscation won't quickly follow, you deserve to have your guns confiscated.

For the rest of us, pay attention. The gun grabbers' seemingly boring rally cries expose their true intentions: to create a nationwide gun registry that can be ready for the day confiscation begins.

The gun grabbers say: "**Gun control can prevent suicides.**"

The truth: There is no evidence that restricting people's access to guns lowers the suicide rate.

The gun grabbers like to conflate suicides that involve guns with violent crimes committed with guns. Doing so is a propaganda effort—plain and simple.

Gun grabbers usually add lines like "Half of all suicides are committed with a gun." The statistic may be true, but it is without any actual meaning.

The reality is that there is no evidence to show that restricting people's access to guns lowers the suicide rate.

Many countries with very strict gun controls have rates of suicide similar to or higher than that of the United States. The U.S. has 14.3 suicides per 100,000 people annually.[357] Meanwhile, Germany's rate is 13.4; Sweden's is 15.4; India's, 15.7; Finland's, 16.3; France's, 16.9; Japan's, 19.7; Poland's, 22.3; and South Korea's, 28.3.[358] Japan has almost no private gun ownership but a much higher suicide rate than the United States.[359]

Yes, there are more guns in America, and therefore people who commit suicide will use them more often. But that doesn't mean more people commit suicide in the United States or that having a gun increases the likelihood of anyone attempting to commit suicide.

It's tragic when a person kills himself. But blaming guns misses the point. Most suicides have one thing in common: the person committing suicide battled some form of mental illness such as depression.

But the gun grabbers make firearms the issue. The government doesn't ban rat poison, rope, tall buildings, or razor blades. Why the double standard for guns?

The gun grabbers say: "Guns kill children. We've got to protect the children!"

The truth: Accidental gun deaths are very rare.

It is always a tragedy when a child's life is cut short. When a child dies in an accident involving a gun, gun grabbers embrace the opportunity to push for more gun control. But we must be on guard that those senseless tragedies do not result in the erosion of our individual liberties.

The obligation to protect children from dangers in the home falls on the parents. A responsible parent will take steps to make his house safe for kids. If parents leave a loaded gun, household chemicals or their prescription drugs within reach of a child, it's their fault if a child is injured—not mine, not yours, and not a deficiency in the law. A society of *250 million* mostly responsible, law-abiding adults[360] should not be forced to surrender their freedoms because a few parents are careless.

In any case, let's look at the frequency of accidental gun deaths. According to the Centers for Disease Control and Prevention (CDC), there were 495 accidental gun deaths in the United States in 2016.[361] That covers people of any age. If you include only children (ages zero to seventeen), the number of deaths drops to 104.[362]

By contrast, the CDC reports that in 2016, there were more than twice as many child deaths by poisoning (264)[363] or in fires (269),[364] eight times as many by drowning (848),[365] twelve times as many in accidental suffocations (1,234),[366] and almost *twenty-three* times as many in motor vehicle accidents (2,361).[367]

In his book *The Bias Against Guns*, researcher John R. Lott Jr. reported that more children under five drowned in five-gallon plastic water buckets than children under ten died from any type of accidental gunshot.[368]

Folks, it's time to put safety locks on water buckets.

Let's also look at the "kids and guns" statistics the anti-gun zealots toss about. On its Gun Violence by the Numbers page, Everytown for Gun Safety claims that "Seven children and teens (age 19 or under) are killed with guns in the U.S. on an average day."[369]

Is this true? Are seven kids *not* coming home from school every day to play Nintendo because they were the victims of a cold-blooded killer with a gun?

Of course not.

For starters, Everytown includes suicides in this number, which account for three of the seven deaths.[370] Some of the anti-gun groups have the honesty to admit this, like the Brady Center, which clearly discloses these numbers.[371]

Everytown also includes within the definition of "children" the segment of the population that includes teenage criminals up to age nineteen.[372] Violent crime is largely a young man's game. And it's happening in cities across America, like Indianapolis, Los Angeles, and Chicago.[373] The group Teen Violence Statistics reports that "more than half of the homicides reported in Los Angeles, and more than half of the homicides reported in Chicago, are related to gang violence."[374]

That half the homicides in these cities result from gang violence is an astounding figure. Though anyone's premature death is tragic, this puts the anti-gunners' research and conclusions in perspective.

Next time you run into a gun grabber who passionately insists on the dangers of guns, calmly explain the facts.

Gun grabbers love to blame the gun, not the gunman.

So, ask them: If they really want to keep children safe, why aren't they ready to ban swimming pools, cars, bicycles, and even water buckets?

If they are worried about suicide, why do they think countries with much stricter gun regulations, like Japan, also have much higher suicide rates than the United States?

If they think regulations are the answer, why will an additional law or regulation work better than the thousands of laws and regulations already on the books?

It's easy to demonize guns with appeals to emotion. It's a lot harder to deal with the facts.

Chapter 9
Gun Grabber Myth #7
"The Second Amendment Doesn't Apply to Modern America"

*Somehow this Amendment Is
Different from All the Others in
the Bill of Rights?*

The gun grabbers say: "The Second Amendment confers no individual right to own guns; it merely allows states to keep a militia, which today is the responsibility of the National Guard."

The truth: The Second Amendment, which appears in the Bill of Rights, says unequivocally that "the people" shall have the right to keep and bear arms.

The Second Amendment is controversial in political discussions the way the New England Patriots are controversial among football fans. You either love it or you hate it.

Those who want to limit the rights recognized by the Second Amendment claim they want "common sense" restrictions on the right to bear arms. Or they say they don't really want to confiscate guns, they just want to limit the particular firearms you need to be able to exercise your right.

Defenders of the Second Amendment reject all that, and for one simple reason. The Founders stated very plainly, "the right of the people to keep and bear arms shall not be infringed." The Second Amendment doesn't say you have the right to keep and bear the arms *that you need*. Or you have the right to keep and bear the arms *that some people think make common sense at any particular moment*.

As soon as we allow certain guns to be banned because some group thinks they are too "powerful," reload too quickly, or hold too many bullets, then we open the door to banning all guns based on how people feel about them at any given time. Why? Because all guns essentially function the same way. They all fire bullets, and those bullets can kill people.

And as soon as we allow bans, the Second Amendment will lose its meaning, and its power, and our rights, will cease to exist.

Those rights are just that—*ours*. No matter how often gun grabbers say the Second Amendment just covers militias and had nothing to do with individual rights, the U.S. Supreme Court ruled explicitly—in *District of Columbia v. Heller* (2008)—that "the Second Amendment protects an individual right to possess a firearm unconnected with service in a militia, and to use that arm for traditionally lawful purposes, such as self-defense within the home."

This conclusion is a no-brainer given where the Second Amendment appears: in the Bill of Rights, which lays out constitutionally protected individual rights that the government cannot infringe on. If the Founders intended the Second Amendment to grant powers to state governments, they sure put it in a funny place.

The Second Amendment says that "the people" shall have the right to keep and bear arms. The Fourth, Ninth, and Tenth Amendments also refer to "the people," and the Supreme Court has made it clear again and again that the term refers to individuals.

Since the Second Amendment stakes out an individual *right* to bear arms, it seems especially odd that the gun grabbers say they can limit that right based on what they think people need at any given time. No one needs protection from self-incrimination if they are innocent, but the Fifth Amendment still provides that protection. No one needs pornography, but the First Amendment still protects it.[375]

In any case, the Founders saw the right to bear arms as a *need*. They made the importance of an armed citizenry abundantly clear because they understood that the first step tyrannical governments take to oppress the citizenry is to disarm them. In April 1775, when the British dispatched armed troops from Boston to the towns of Lexington and Concord, their objective was not to rape and pillage the countryside but to seize the guns the colonists had collected. After winning their independence from Britain, the Framers of the Constitution made certain to protect the right to bear arms in the Second Amendment.

Gun control enthusiasts commonly claim that Second Amendment supporters ignore the amendment's opening clause: "A well regulated militia, being necessary to the security of a free state…." That's not true. Second Amendment supporters just understand the meaning of "well regulated militia" and reject efforts to redefine the phrase based on modern language usage.

"Well regulated," in the Second Amendment, has nothing to do with government regulation as we know it today. The words actually refer to men being trained and proficient with firearms so as to be able to defend their family, community, and/or state.[376]

"Militia" is the other word the gun grabbers make hay with. They point to the word and announce, "See? The Second Amendment says that the right to bear arms exists only in the context of serving in the militia. So it's talking about state-sanctioned military service—you know, what the National Guard handles today."

This is wrong too. And to understand why, you don't need to wade through all the court decisions and legal analysis on the subject. (I've done that, so you don't have to!)

Here are the essential points you need to know:

First, the Framers of the Constitution didn't understand "militia" to describe only official, state-sanctioned military units. Many of them spoke of the militia as referring to the entire adult male population. After all, the Minutemen who stood up to the British at Lexington and Concord were a group of townsmen.

Second, as the late Justice Antonin Scalia explained in the Supreme Court's *Heller* decision, the phrase "well regulated militia" is part of what's called a prefatory clause, which was common at the time the Second Amendment was drafted.[377] A prefatory clause doesn't *restrict* the meaning of the main or operative clause; all it does is explain the purpose of the operative clause. In Justice Scalia's words: "[t]he Second Amendment's prefatory clause announces the purpose for which the right was codified: to prevent elimination of the militia. The prefatory clause does not suggest that preserving the militia was the only reason Americans valued the ancient right; most undoubtedly thought it was even more important for self-defense and hunting."[378]

Recognizing this history, the U.S. Department of Justice in 2004 issued a 103-page report, with 437 footnotes, concluding that "the Second Amendment secures an individual right to keep and bear arms" and "a right of individuals generally, not a right of states or a right restricted to persons serving in militias."[379]

After the March for Our Lives rallies, retired Supreme Court Justice John Paul Stevens got a lot of attention for his *New York Times* op-ed headlined "Repeal the Second Amendment."[380] Gun grabbers cheered.

But think about what Justice Stevens is saying. Even as he voices full-throated opposition to gun rights, he acknowledges that the Second Amendment stands as a roadblock the gun grabbers simply can't get around.

The gun grabbers say: "The Second Amendment allows for common sense gun regulations."

The truth: Yes, the Second Amendment does leave room for certain gun regulations—but how are you defining "common sense"?

No right is absolute. All rights have limits. You can't yell "Fire" in a crowded theater.

We've all heard these arguments. They're all true! But they are *philosophical* arguments that don't help us grapple with the reality of the government trying to limit *your* and my freedoms to defend our lives and protect our families.

Sure, there are limits to rights, but those limits govern actions. We do not try to prevent people from yelling fire in a theater by restricting people's access to the theater or hampering their ability to speak. We apply rules of conduct for a civilized society that we expect people to follow, and we punish them when they break those rules.

Look at an example of the "commonsense" regulation the gun grabbers demand: universal background checks. This is the first goal listed in the March for Our Lives mission statement.

As we saw in the previous chapter, we already *have* background checks. And here's an additional point that usually gets lost amid the fevered cries for background checks: they haven't done anything to stop mass killers.

Even *The New York Times* admits this. In an article updated after the Parkland shootings, the *Times* conceded, "A vast majority of guns used in 19 recent mass shootings were bought legally and with a federal background check."[381] Private transfers (the famous "gun show loophole") were not the problem and extending background checks to cover private transfers would not have prevented any of these criminal acts.

The gun grabbers are calling for a "solution" that we know (and they know) won't solve the problem.

Here we see the massive hole in the gun grabbers' argument. They always call for more laws. They demand that Congress "take action" to stop the killings.

But they can never answer a simple question: If the thousands of gun laws and regulations already on the books haven't kept criminals and crazies from killing large numbers of people, what makes them think that one more law will solve everything? Especially when that "new" law is just a tweaking, a minor alteration, of something already in effect—a law that hasn't stopped determined criminals.

That's the hard truth about the "commonsense" gun restrictions we hear about: They won't work. Worse, they'll infringe on our rights and freedoms.

Don't be fooled. You should never give away your right to defend yourself and those you care about. Once this right is gone, you will never get it back.

And if you lose this right, you won't be able to employ the one true "common sense" response to violent criminals: having a gun and knowing how to use it.

The gun grabbers don't want you to have that right. Just look at what happened to the Parkland student who came out in full support of the Second Amendment. Broward Police harassed him because he went to a gun range with his father to learn how to lawfully use and respect firearms.[382]

The gun grabbers say: "The Second Amendment applies only to muskets."

The truth: If the Framers had intended the Second Amendment to apply only to muskets, they would have used that word.

Here is another line the gun grabbers use on cable TV, talk radio, Twitter, and left-wing websites. A typical headline, from *Ozy.com* (which bills itself as "a daily digital magazine custom built for the Change Generation"): "Why the 2nd Amendment Applies Only to Your Muskets and Dueling Pistols."[383]

This is really a more specific iteration of a myth I debunked in an earlier chapter: that the Founders didn't envision modern firearms so the Second Amendment doesn't protect these dangerous weapons.

As discussed in that chapter, the Founders understood that technology advances rapidly, and they intentionally kept the language of the Constitution from being too restrictive to accommodate that kind of development. Arguing that the Second Amendment applies only to muskets makes as much sense as saying the First Amendment applies only to people handing out pamphlets drafted by Publius while standing on a soap box.

If the Framers really wanted to protect only muskets, they would have used the word *muskets*. Again, as we have seen, plenty of other kinds of firearms existed when the Founders drafted the Bill of Rights, including a rifle magazine that could hold twenty rounds of ammunition.[384]

The U.S. Supreme Court has dispensed with this myth—unanimously so.

In 2016, the Court considered a case in which a Massachusetts woman was convicted for carrying a stun gun for self-defense.[385] The Massachusetts Supreme Judicial Court, always in the liberal legal vanguard, upheld the woman's conviction claiming a stun gun "is not the type of weapon that is eligible for Second Amendment protection" because it was "not in common use at the time of [the Second Amendment's] enactment."[386]

The U.S. Supreme Court unanimously vacated the woman's conviction, dismissing the Massachusetts court's reasoning.[387] The Supreme Court's ruling pointed back to its *Heller* decision, which says that the Second Amendment "extends, prima facie, to all instruments that constitute bearable arms, even those that were not in existence at the time of the founding."[388]

In a concurring opinion, Justice Samuel Alito pointed to *Heller* too. Justice Alito cited the part of the Court's ruling that rejected as "bordering on the frivolous" the argument "that only those arms in existence in the 18th century are protected by the Second Amendment."[389]

Not a lot of wiggle room for the gun grabbers here.

Except they still try to find some. So now they argue that the Second Amendment was never intended to protect individual gun ownership and that the Supreme Court cooked up this new interpretation in *Heller*.

Not surprisingly, this claim is bogus too. *Heller* simply affirmed what people believed for more than two hundred years: that the Second Amendment guarantees an individual right to bear arms.[390] Before *Heller*, the Court had never ruled to uphold a law to prevent people from purchasing guns, with the only exception being if someone lost their right to bear arms for cause (felony conviction, mental illness, and so forth).

The gun grabbers say: "Guns are no defense against governmental tyranny."

The truth: Er, have you read any history?

The anti-gunners say that no ordinary group of Americans could stop a tyrannical government in the era of drones, nuclear weapons, and the great power of the U.S. military. So, practically speaking, how does the right to keep and bear arms prevent tyranny in the modern era?

History is full of cases where rebel fighters with less powerful firearms took on, held off, and in many cases defeated a much larger and more powerful military.

The American Revolution was won against the greatest military force then in the world, *i.e.*, the British Empire.

Didn't the United States lose the Vietnam War to an enemy armed with mostly small arms?[391] Let's not forget Afghanistan and Iraq either. The United States had a heck of a time subduing enemies who were armed mostly with small arms.

If you want to find out how tyrants feel about the private ownership of firearms, just ask them.

Adolf Hitler said in 1942, "The most foolish mistake we could possibly make would be to allow the subjugated races to possess arms."[392] It's uncertain what Hitler meant by "subjugated races." Perhaps he was talking about the Poles. Or the Czechs. Or the Belgians. Or the French. Or the Norwegians. Or the Dutch. Or the gays. Or the Jews.... Hitler's Germany killed about eleven million non-combatants alone.[393]

A young and energetic Mao Zedong said in 1938, "Every Communist must grasp the truth, 'Political power grows out of the barrel of a gun,'" and "Our principle is that the [Communist] Party commands the gun, and the gun must never be allowed to command the Party."[394] Sounds legit.... Mao's regime killed at least forty-five million Chinese.[395]

Benito Mussolini told the Italian Senate in 1923, "On the morrow of each conflict I gave the categorical order to confiscate the largest possible number of weapons of every sort and kind."[396]

Joseph Stalin made things pretty clear when he said, "If the opposition disarms—well and good. If it refuses to disarm—we shall disarm it ourselves."[397] Stalin's Soviet government killed over five million Soviet citizens.[398]

If you doubt the importance of private gun ownership as a foil against tyranny, just ask yourself why pretty much every mass-murdering tyrant of the twentieth century wanted the people disarmed.

Or just ask Nobel Prize winner Aleksandr Solzhenitsyn, imprisoned in the gulag under Stalin.

Consider the reflections he recorded in *The Gulag Archipelago*:

> And how we burned in the camps later, thinking: What would things have been like if every Security operative, when he went out at night to make an arrest, had been uncertain whether he would return alive and had to say good-bye to his family? Or if, during periods of mass arrests, as for example in Leningrad, when they arrested a quarter of the entire city, people had not simply sat there in their lairs, paling with terror at every bang of the downstairs door and at every step on the staircase, but had understood they had nothing left to lose and had boldly set up in the downstairs hall an ambush of half a dozen people with axes, hammers, pokers, or whatever else was at hand?.... The Organs would very quickly have suffered a shortage of officers and transport and, notwithstanding all of Stalin's thirst, the cursed machine would have ground to a halt! If...if...We didn't love freedom enough. And even more—we had no awareness of the real situation.[399]

Judge Alex Kozinski had it right in his dissenting opinion in the 2003 case *Silveira v. Lockyer*. Kozinski, a judge on the U.S. Ninth Circuit Court of Appeals, hit the nail on head when he reflected on some of our more sordid American history: "[T]he simple truth—born of experience—is that tyranny thrives best where government need not fear the wrath of an armed people. Our own sorry history bears this out: Disarmament was the tool of choice for subjugating both slaves and free blacks in the South. In Florida, patrols searched blacks' homes for weapons, confiscated those found and punished their owners without judicial process."[400]

It's a little scary to read that Judge Kozinski regards the Second Amendment as sort of a "doomsday provision, one designed for those exceptionally rare circumstances where all other rights have failed."[401] But those circumstances have happened throughout modern human history, and we should do what we can to make sure it doesn't happen in America.

I once heard this comment: "I saw a movie where only the military and police had guns. It was called *Schindler's List*."

It's true: Nazi Germany disarmed its citizens. Not all at once, but incrementally.[402] It began with the registration of firearms before the Nazis came to power.[403] Understand that registering a gun is like registering your car, meaning that the government knows who owns every car and where those cars are located. Same with the guns in Germany.

Knowing the owner and location of every gun in Germany came in very handy a few years later when the Nazis took power. They used this information to confiscate firearms from anybody the Nazi Party distrusted, starting with the Jews.[404] Gun confiscation continued, expanding to people who were "politically unreliable."[405]

Eventually, and with few exceptions for loyal Nazis, gun ownership was limited to the police and the government—which is exactly what the gun grabbers advocate for now.[406]

Students of history will recall that went poorly.

Conclusion

What's Your Plan?

When it comes to guns, what do the data show us?

What does the *smart money* do for self-defense?

What do the billionaires, the "1 percent," choose?

What does Michael Bloomberg choose for *his* own protection?

What does the Secret Service choose for protecting the president?

Do these groups depend on hope and wishful thinking? Of course not.

Mark Zuckerberg spends $20,000 a day—*a day!*—on security. He doesn't depend on signs that say "Gun-Free Zone."

You shouldn't either!

And since you're never likely to have your own phalanx of armed security guards, you should jealously guard your right to carry arms for your own defense and the defense of your family.

Trusting your life to the next Scot Peterson, that disgraced Parkland public servant, should be a risk you want to avoid.

The right to bear arms is simply the right to the most efficient and practical means of self-defense against criminal predators and tyrannical governments to everything in between.

If you're a woman, this right is doubly important for you. Women on average have 40 percent less upper body strength than men.[407] So unless you have the powers of Gal Gadot's *Wonder Woman* or Scarlett Johansson's *Black Widow*, you have a small chance of fighting off a bigger, stronger male attacker (or attackers).

How many *#MeToo* attacks might have been stopped had the victim brandished a .38 Special or a 9mm Glock?

Can you name another sensible self-defense alternative that comes close to a gun?

It's always been better to be a survivor than a victim. Or, as they say, it's better to be in a shootout than a massacre.

"Everyone Has a Plan Until They Get Punched in the Mouth"

At the beginning of this book I told you my aim was to do two things:

- strip bare how young people like the Parkland students have been duped and are being exploited for political gain and to short-circuit any legitimate debate, and

- lay out the truth about guns and safety that you won't hear in all the emotion-drenched media coverage.

Now that you've seen how the gun control movement works, taken a close look at the gun grabbers' assertions, and considered the facts, I want to leave you with one more thing.

I want to leave you with this question: *What's your plan?*

Seriously, ask yourself: What is your plan for defending yourself and your loved ones?

The great American philosopher Mike Tyson said, "Everyone has a plan until they get punched in the mouth."[408]

The scary thing is that when it comes to self-defense, few people even have a plan.

What will you do if a criminal invades your home? Or attacks you on the street or in a parking garage? Or opens fire in your community? What will you do if your neighborhood becomes a hot spot for riots or looting? How will you defend yourself and your loved ones from the local MS-13 chapter?

These scenarios may seem unlikely. But there are nearly as many violent crimes in the United States every year as there are fires.[409] Many people have plans for what they'll do in the event of a fire. Schools, businesses, and even many families conduct fire safety drills. After 9/11, it became commonplace for schools, businesses, and families to have an emergency response plan in place in the event of a terrorist attack.

So why wouldn't you come up with a plan for protecting yourself from violent thugs?

Think of it as being prepared. Buying a gun and getting trained to use it is like buying fire extinguishers, wearing seat belts, keeping extra bottled water in your pantry, having an alarm system, and buying homeowner's insurance.

Of course, you hope that nothing bad will ever happen and that you'll never need any of those things.

But bad things do happen, and it's best to be ready before they do.

You need to plan if your burglar alarm ever goes off.

If you don't think you want a gun, that's okay. Gun rights advocates don't want to require anyone to carry a firearm. To be *pro-gun* is to be *pro-choice*.

But if you pass on owning a gun, what *is* your plan? Will you simply rely on the good nature of the criminal who has already decided to break into your home to "do the right thing," *or* do you plan to call 911 and have someone else armed with a gun show up to protect you?

Call 911? Okay, but remember, the police aren't really "first responders." Maybe they're minutes away, but a criminal needs just a second or two.

Ultimately, your only protection is to have a realistic plan to defend yourself.

The Depth of the Problems

School shootings are tragedies. They are horrifying. No one wants to see repeats of such wanton and senseless violence.

Everyone can agree on that.

The disagreements come when we have to determine causes and cast blame, and decide how to stop future attacks.

The anti-gun crowd offers a simplistic analysis: "*Ban Guns!*"[410] And so they want to punish the millions of law-abiding gun owners in America who had absolutely nothing to do with the crimes.

The truth is more complex, which probably makes it harder for a lot of people to stomach. The school shooting tragedies have resulted from a range of failures—especially the failures of schools, the mental health system, and law enforcement to pick up on warning signs and prevent the horrible crimes that occurred.

The United States faces many problems that must be solved.

The U.S. has a problem of *mental illness violence* and no sensible strategy to address it.

The U.S. has a gang violence problem and hasn't found a workable strategy to address it.

The U.S. criminal justice system releases prisoners every day, some 70 percent of whom will reoffend.[411]

The U.S. has some number of Islamic radicals who would like to kill as many infidels as possible.

Somehow, the gun grabbers reduce all this to: *We need more gun control!*

Even though *thousands* of gun laws and regulations haven't prevented these tragedies.

Even though most of the proposed new gun restrictions *wouldn't* have prevented these tragedies.

Even though violent criminals will always find a way to commit violence. (Just ask Britain, France, China, Brazil...)

Even though "gun-free zones" are where virtually all mass shootings have occurred.

Even though states with the highest rates of gun ownership also have some of the lowest homicide death rates.

Even though "when guns are outlawed, only outlaws have guns," — or perhaps even worse, only the government.

"You First"

You have a choice to make in the battle for gun rights.

You can listen to David Hogg and his fellow Parkland survivors who support gun control. They endured a searing experience. They speak forcefully. They are passionate.

But they are wrong.

Sure, they and the anti-gun activists who support them employ a rhetorical device that is hard to argue with: they "demand action." Who could be against "action"?

Well, it matters what the "action" is. At some point you must explain why the particular set of actions you call for will solve the problems you've identified.

And on that front, the gun grabbers fail.

If you want to listen to them, that's your choice. Just remember, their plan is to take away *your* right and ability to defend yourself and your family.

And once you have given away this right, you will *never* get it back.

Endnotes

1 Barack Obama, "Parkland Students" TIME Most Influential People 2018, April 19, 2018, http://time.com/collection/most-influential-people-2018/5217568/parkland-students/

2 "PARKLAND STUDENTS SHINE, J.LO BUSTS A MOVE AT TIME 100 GALA" *New York Post Page Six*, April 26, 2015, https://pagesix.com/2018/04/25/parkland-students-shine-j-lo-busts-a-move-at-time-100-gala/?utm_source=maropost&utm_medium=email&utm_campaign=pagesixdaily&utm_content=20180426&mpweb=755-6693030-719149016

3 Ibid.

4 "Former White House staff emails reveal private thoughts amid one of the nation's most horrific school tragedies," *The Baltimore Post*, May 23, 2018, http://thebaltimorepost.com/former-white-house-staff-emails-reveal-private-thoughts-amid-one-of-the-nations-most-horrific-school-tragedies/

5 "A Terrible Thing to Waste," *The New York Times Magazine*, July 31, 2009, https://www.nytimes.com/2009/08/02/magazine/02FOB-onlanguage-t.html

6 "Women's March organizers are planning a national student walkout to protest gun violence," CNN, February 18, 2018, https://www.cnn.com/2018/02/18/us/national-student-walkout-womens-march-trnd/index.html; "Women's March group calls for national school walkout over gun control," *The Hill*, February 17, 2018, http://thehill.com/blogs/blog-briefing-room/news/374359-womens-march-group-calls-for-national-school-walkout-over-gun "A Generation Raised on Gun Violence Sends a Loud Message to Adults:

Enough," CNN, March 16, 2018,
https://www.cnn.com/2018/03/14/us/national-school-
walkout-gun-violence-protests/index.html

[7] "The Top Five Worst Speeches at the Women's March on
Washington," *National Review*, January 24, 2017,
https://www.nationalreview.com/2017/01/womens-march-
speeches-marked-left-wing-extremism-social-justice/; "The
very mixed messages from an unwelcoming march," *The
Washington Times*, January 26, 2017,
https://m.washingtontimes.com /news/2017/jan/26/the-
very-mixed-messages-from-an-unwelcoming-march/; "12
Things We Saw At The Women's March In Washington
DC," *The Federalist*, January 22, 2017, http://the
federalist.com/2017/01/22/heres-what-we-saw-at-the-
womens-march-in-washington-d-c/

[8] "How Madonna Gave Trump Ammo With a Cry for Peace," *The
Atlantic*, January 23, 2017,
https://www.theatlantic.com/entertainment/archive/2017/01
/madonna-trump-blow-up-the-white-house-womens-
march-speech/514106/

[9] Dr. Susan Berry, "Teachers Unions Support Student Walkouts as
'Protest to Change Gun Laws,'" *Breitbart*, March 13, 2018,
http://www.breitbart.com/big-
government/2018/03/13/teachers-unions-support-student-
walkouts-as-protest-to-change-gun-laws/

[10] "Planned Student Walkouts Draw Varied Responses From
Oregon Schools," *OPB*, March 13, 2018,
https://www.opb.org/news/article/student-walkout-protest-
oregon-portland-eugene-salem-pendleton/; "Utah schools
make plans to handle student walkouts," Fox13, March 9,
2018, http://fox13now.com/2018/03/09/utah-schools-make-
plans-to-handle-student-walkouts/; "Oakland County
students plan walkouts Wednesday in support of gun
control," Oakland Press, March 12, 2018,
http://www.theoaklandpress.com/general-
news/20180312/oakland-county-students-plan-walkouts-
wednesday-in-support-of-gun-control; "Brattleboro Union
High School students demand change," *Brattleboro Reformer*,

March 14, 2018, http://www.reformer.com/stories/students-demand-change,534629

[11] Ben Shapiro, "READ: Emails From High School Students Who Oppose Today's Massive Gun Control Walkout," *Daily Wire*, March 14, 2018, https://www.dailywire.com/news/28224/read-emails-high-school-students-who-oppose-todays-ben-shapiro

[12] "U.S. Students Stage Massive Walkout to Protest Gun Violence," Associated Press, March 15, 2018, https://www.apnews.com/c183323b5e6546419ae08b8c469b065a/US-students-stage-massive-walkout-to-protest-gun-violence; "Thousands of students walk out of school in nationwide gun violence protest," *The Washington Post*, March 14, 2018, https://www.washingtonpost.com/news/education/wp/2018/03/14/students-have-just-had-enough-walkouts-planned-across-the-nation-one-month-after-florida-shooting/?noredirect=on&utm_term=.3d573e12a676

[13] "High school enrollment in the U.S. from 1965 to 2014 for public and private schools with projections up to 2026 (in 1,000)," *Statista*, https://www.statista.com/statistics/183996/us-high-school-enrollment-in-public-and-private-institutions/; National Center for Education Statistics, https://nces.ed.gov/fastfacts/display. asp?id=372

[14] "Brattleboro Union High School students demand change," *Brattleboro Reformer*, March 14, 2018, http://www.reformer.com/stories/students-demand-change,534629 (noting about 250 students walked out); compare http://buhs.wsesu.org/about.html (high school has about 900 students).

[15] "Who's Paying (to) "March for Our Lives?" Capital Research Center, March 28, 2018, https://capitalresearch.org/article/whos-paying-to-march-for-our-lives/

[16] "Steven Spielberg & Jeffrey Katzenberg Among Hillary Clinton's $1M SuperPAC Donors," *Deadline Hollywood*, July

31, 2015, http://deadline.com/2015/07/hillary-clinton-steven-spielberg-jeffrey-katzenberg-donars-1201488889/; "George Clooney endorses Hillary Clinton and says she's 'the only grown-up in the room,'" *Business Insider*, March 21, 2016, http://www.businessinsider.com/george-clooney-hillary-clinton-endorsement-2016-3; "Oprah endorses Hillary Clinton," *Politico*, June 16, 2016, https://www.politico.com/story/2016/06/oprah-winfrey-endorses-clinton-224408; "Salesforce CEO, Marc Benioff, backs Hillary Clinton," *CNN Money*, March 7, 2016, http://money.cnn.com/2016/03/07/news/companies/salesforce-ceo-hillary-clinton/index.html

[17] Rhetoric, by Aristotle, The Internet Classics Archive, MIT, http://classics.mit.edu/Aristotle/rhetoric.1.i.html

[18] "2 Parkland Students With Gunshot Injuries Plan To Sue School District, Officials," *Huffington Post*, March 6, 2018, https://www.huffingtonpost.com/entry/2-injured-parkland-students-announce-plans-to-sue-district_us_5a9ee8ece4b0d4f5b66b0b58; "Pro-Gun Parkland Student Kyle Kashuv: Why Wasn't I Invited To Speak At The March?" *Real Clear Politics*, March 25, 2018, https://www.realclearpolitics.com/video/2018/03/25/pro-gun_parkland_student_kyle_kashuv_why_wasnt_i_invited_to_speak_at_the_march.html

[19] "Obama praises Parkland students in *TIME*, 'Our children are calling us to account,'" *USA Today*, April 19, 2018, https://www.usatoday.com/story/news/politics/onpolitics/2018/04/19/obama-praises-parkland-students-time-magazine-our-children-calling-us-account/532604002/

[20] "David Hogg is Mad as Hell," *The Outline*, March 5, 2018, https://theoutline.com/post/3571/david-hogg-parkland-interview?zd=3&zi=3qodkqns

[21] Ibid.

[22] Ibid.

[23] Ibid.

[24] Ibid.

[25] "Parkland's David Hogg: Rules Requiring Clear Backpacks Violate Our First Amendment Rights," YouTube, March 24, 2018, https://www.youtube.com/watch?v=dEQbjUGEyGc

[26] "She Claims That She Was a 'Pawn' Who Was Tricked by Lawyers Seeking to Legalize Abortion. This Is Her Shocking Story," *The Blaze*, January 22, 2016, https://www.theblaze.com/news/2016/01/22/she-claims-that-she-was-a-pawn-who-was-tricked-by-lawyers-seeking-to-legalize-abortion-this-is-her-shocking-story

[27] Ibid.

[28] Ibid.

[29] Ibid.

[30] Ibid.

[31] "'If we have data, let's look at data. If all we have are our opinions, let's go with mine' Why data matters in a membership organization," The Association of Theological Schools, https://www.ats.edu/blog/data-matters/%E2%80%9Cif-we-have-data-lets-look-data-if-all-we-have-are-our-opinions-lets-go-mine%E2%80%9D-why-data-matters-0

[32] Ibid.

[33] "It cost $20,000 a day to protect Mark Zuckerberg," *CNBC Inside Wealth*, April 16, 2018, https://www.cnbc.com/2018/04/16/it-cost-20000-a-day-to-protect-mark-zuckerberg.html

[34] "In post about Las Vegas shooting, Mark Zuckerberg addresses gun control debate," *Mashable*, October 2, 2017, https://mashable.com/2017/10/02/zuckerberg-statement-las-vegas-shooting/#BhL9Hh55C5qQ

[35] "Is Facebook blocking posts about guns?" *Connecting Vets*, March 2, 2018, http://connectingvets.com/articles/facebook-blocking-posts-about-guns

[36] "7 Liberal Hypocrites Who Call For Gun Control While Being Protected By Guns," *Townhall*, March 23, 2013,

https://townhall.com/columnists/johnhawkins/2013/03/23/7
-liberal-hypocrites-who-call-for-gun-control-while-being-
protected-by-guns-n1546898

[37] "Oscars Security: LAPD Will Have Over 500 Officers On Hand at Red Carpet," *Variety*, March 2, 2018, http://variety.com/2018/film/awards/oscars-security-2018-red-carpet-1202716110/

[38] "Musicians Add 'Counterterrorism Briefing' to Pre-Grammy Schedule," *Rolling Stone*, January 26, 2018, https://www.rollingstone.com/music/news/musicians-add-counterterrorism-briefing-to-pre-grammy-schedule-w515827

[39] "George Clooney has installed James Bond worthy security at his home," *Marie Claire*, August 11, 2017, http://www.marieclaire.co.uk/news/celebrity-news/george-clooney-home-security-528976

[40] "Oprah Winfrey's Bodyguards Rough Up Indian Journalists," *Hollywood Reporter*, January 20, 2012, https://www.hollywoodreporter.com/news/oprah-winfreys-bodyguards-rough-up-283520

[41] "Spielberg recounts fears, anguish over alleged stalker," CNN, February 26, 1998, http://www.cnn.com/SHOWBIZ/9802/26/spielberg.stalker/

[42] "Maybe don't roll your eyes at Kim Kardashian's gun control stance," *Yahoo Lifestyle*, February 16, 2018, https://www.yahoo.com/lifestyle/maybe-dont-roll-eyes-kim-kardashians-gun-control-stance-200033650.html; "Kris Jenner says the Kardashians are protected by armed guards, *New York Post Page Six*, June 13, 2017, https://pagesix.com/2017/06/13/kris-jenner-says-the-kardashians-are-protected-by-armed-guards/

[43] "EXCLUSIVE: How Sylvester Stallone was accused of sexually assaulting a 16-year-old fan: Police report reveals girl claimed star made her give him and his bodyguard oral sex and threatened they would 'beat her head in' if she ever told," *Daily Mail*, November 16, 2017,

http://www.dailymail.co.uk/news/article-5081605/Sylvester-Stallone-accused-forcing-teen-threesome.html

[44] "Ariana Grande Delivers Emotional Performance Of 'Be Alright' At March For Our Lives," *Hollywood Life*, March 24, 2018, http://hollywoodlife.com/2018/03/24/ariana-grande-sings-be-alright-march-for-our-lives-performance-video/; "Ariana Grande keeps a low profile as she touches down in Rio De Janeiro with her entourage... after resuming tour in South America following devastating Manchester attack," *Daily Mail*, June 28, 2017, http://www.dailymail.co.uk/tvshowbiz/article-4647356/Ariana-Grande-flanked-bodyguards-Rio-airport.html

[45] "Jennifer Lawrence Speaks Out Against Gun Violence and In Support of Florida Shooting Survivors," *Elle*, February 27, 2018, https://www.elle.com/culture/career-politics/a18818357/jennifer-lawrence-gun-violence-florida-shooting/; "Hot celebrity bodyguards From Kim Kardashian's dishy security to Kylie Jenner's Gucci carrying hunk," *Glamour*, June 23, 2017, http://www.glamourmagazine.co.uk/gallery/hot-celebrity-bodyguards-jennifer-lawrence

[46] Ibid.; "Lady Gaga leads stars urging gun control measures after Las Vegas carnage," *The Telegraph*, October 2, 2017, https://www.telegraph.co.uk/news/2017/10/02/lady-gaga-urges-gun-control-celebrities-voice-shock-las-vegas/

[47] Ibid.; "Chelsea Handler, Kristen Stewart Urge Public to Stand Up Against Gun Violence," *People*, June 8, 2017, http://people.com/celebrity/kristen-stewart-chelsea-handler-gun-violence/

[48] Ibid.; "Taylor Swift and Selena Gomez speak out in support of gun control," *The Independent*, March 23, 2018, https://www.independent.co.uk/arts-entertainment/music/taylor-swift-selena-gomez-march-for-our-lives-gun-control-instagram-support-a8271326.html

[49] Ibid.; 'Lady Gaga, Miranda, Britney Spears sign open letter on gun control," *USA Today*, June 23, 2016,

https://www.usatoday.com/story/life/people/2016/06/23/lady
-gaga-lin-manuelo-miranda-britney-spears-sign-open-letter-
on-gun-control/86279230/

50 Ibid.; "Lady Gaga, Katy Perry, and More Sign Open Letter to
Congress Demanding Gun Control," *Vanity Fair*, June 23,
2016, https://www.vanityfair.com/style/2016/06/billboard-
gun-control-open-letter

51 Ibid.; "25 CELEBRITIES DEMANDING GUN
CONTROL: BEYONCÉ, CHER, ADAM LAMBERT &
MORE," Fuse TV, February 26, 2018,
https://www.fuse.tv/2016/06/gun-control-celebrities-list

52 "Amy Schumer Increases Personal Security While Pushing Gun
Control for Americans," *Breitbart*, September 2. 2016,
http://www.breitbart.com/big-hollywood/2016/09/02/amy-
schumer-increases-security-pushing-gun-control/

53 "If The Shoe Fits, You're a Dumb Ass Gun Banner,"
AmmoLand, May 11, 2018,
https://www.ammoland.com/2018/05/if-the-shoe-fits-
dumb-ass/#ixzz5GGCdfBOM "ROSIE: MY GUARDS
ARE ARMED, BUT NOT IN HOUSE," *New York Post*,
June 1, 2000, https://nypost.com/2000/06/01/rosie-my-
guards-are-armed-but-not-in-house/

54 "Brad Pitt and Angelina Jolie's Shocking Stand On Gun
Control – Obama Must Be Livid!" *Halls of Karma*, June 20,
2016, https://hallsofkarma.us/2016/06/20/brad-pitt-and-
angelina-jolies-shocking-stand-on-gun-control-obama-
must-be-livid/

55 "NYC's Michael Bloomberg accused of 'hypocrisy' for arming
security detail in gun-free Bermuda," *The Washington Times*,
March 26, 2013,
https://www.washingtontimes.com/news/2013/mar/26/nycs-
michael-bloomberg-accused-hypocrisy-arming-se/

56 "Jackie Mason: Bloomberg, With 12 Armed Bodyguards, Is a
Hypocrite on Gun Control," *Newsmax*, February 14, 2016,
https://www.newsmax.com/newsfront/jackie-mason-
bloomberg-hypocrite-gun-control/2016/02/14/id/714326/

[57] "Seahawks Owner Paul Allen Gives $1M to Gun Control Ballot Initiative," *Bleacher Report*, https://bleacherreport.com/articles/2777191-blazers-owner-paul-allen-contributes-1m-on-gun-control-ballot-initiative

[58] "Seahawks owner Paul Allen, sister settle as bodyguards claim smuggling, bribery," *Seattle Post-Intelligencer*, November 12, 2013, https://www.seattlepi.com/seattlenews/article/Seahawks-owner-Paul-Allen-sister-settle-as-4978500.php

[59] Ibid.

[60] Ibid.

[61] "The Vice President's Lucrative Deal with the Secret Service," Fox News Radio, April 14, 2015, https://radio.foxnews.com/2015/04/14/the-vice-presidents-lucrative-deal-with-the-secret-service/

[62] "Obama revives his 'cling to guns or religion' analysis — for Donald Trump supporters," *The Washington Post*, December 21, 2015, https://www.washingtonpost.com/news/the-fix/wp/2015/12/21/obama-dusts-off-his-cling-to-guns-or-religion-idea-for-donald-trump/?utm_term=.af0b0b1f166b

[63] "Obama signs bill, gets Secret Service protection for life," *CNN Politics*, January 10, 2013, http://politicalticker.blogs.cnn.com/2013/01/10/obama-signs-bill-gets-secret-service-protection-for-life/

[64] "Photos: Hillary Builds a Wall... Around Her House," *Townhall*, August 12, 2016, https://townhall.com/tipsheet/justinholcomb/2016/08/12/photos-hillary-builds-a-wall-around-her-house-n2204239

[65] "Armed guards protect Senate Democrats as they demand new gun-control laws," *The Washington Times*, October 8, 2015, https://www.washingtontimes.com/news/2015/oct/8/armed-guards-protect-senate-democrats-they-demand-/

[66] "Sen. Feinstein no longer has concealed weapon permit," *The Hill*, December 20, 2012, http://thehill.com/blogs/blog-briefing-room/news/273989-feinstein-doesnt-have-concealed-carry-permit-anymore; "Dianne Feinstein Talks

Guns, Opens Up About Her Own Firearm Ownership," *Huffington Post*, April 3, 2013, https://www.huffingtonpost.com/2013/04/03/dianne-feinstein-guns_n_3010058.html

[67] "Feinstein, Pelosi among richest in Congress," *SF Gate*, October 5, 2012, https://www.sfgate.com/politics/article/Feinstein-Pelosi-among-richest-in-Congress-3924070.php

[68] "A Who's Who List of Agencies Guarding the Powerful," *The New York Times*, April 12, 2017, https://www.nytimes.com/2017/04/12/us/politics/secret-service-protection-washington.html

[69] "Members have 24-hour protection at Capitol but home is a different story," *The Hill*, April 23, 2013, http://thehill.com/capital-living/cover-stories/295415-lawmaker-security

[70] "'They do royal weddings. We do schoolkids' funerals': *New York Daily News'* chilling front page sparks applause and outrage," *Daily Mirror*, May 20, 2018, https://www.mirror.co.uk/news/world-news/they-royal-weddings-schoolkids-funerals-12566722

[71] "Here's what you should know about Texas gun laws," *Caller Times*, May 18, 2018, https://www.caller.com/story/news/local/texas/state-bureau/2018/05/18/what-you-should-know-texas-gun-laws/624655002/

[72] "Windsor is on lock down with anti-terror bollards as police and military prepare for the Royal wedding dress rehearsal starting at 9am on Thursday," *Daily Mail*, May 15, 2018, http://www.dailymail.co.uk/news/article-5730961/Windsor-beefs-security-ahead-royal-wedding-final-preparations-place.html

[73] "The royal wedding costs an estimated $42.8 million—and 94% of it is for security," CNBC, May 19, 2018, https://www.cnbc.com/2018/05/18/the-royal-wedding-may-cost-43-million-and-94-percent-of-that-is-for-security.html

[74] "The Pope Has A Small But Deadly Army Of Elite Warriors Protecting Him," *Foxtrot Alpha*, September 28, 2015, https://foxtrotalpha.jalopnik.com/the-pope-has-a-small-but-deadly-army-of-elite-warriors-1733268646; "POPE FRANCIS: AFTER U.S. GUN CONTROL MARCHES, CHURCH LEADER WANTS YOUTH TO KEEP SHOUTING," *Newsweek*, March 25, 2018, http://www.newsweek.com/pope-francis-after-march-our-lives-church-leader-wants-youth-keep-shouting-859735

[75] "How the Catholic Church could help lead a gun control movement," *America The Jesuit Review*, February 21, 2018, https://www.americamagazine.org/politics-society/2018/02/21/how-catholic-church-could-help-lead-gun-control-movement

[76] "Security Stepped Up Across New York City For Christmas," *CBS New York*, December 25, 2017, http://newyork.cbslocal.com/2017/12/25/christmas-security-nyc/

[77] "College Feminists Are Terrified That Sam Colt Really Might Make Them Equal," *Bearing Arms*, February 20, 2015, https://bearingarms.com/bob-o/2015/02/20/college-feminists-terrified-sam-colt-really-might-make-equal/; Barry Popik, "Be not afraid of any man, no matter what his size; when danger threatens… I will equalize," February 24, 2013, https://www.barrypopik.com/index.php/new_york_city/entry/be_not_afraid_of_any_man_no_matter_what_his_size_when_danger_threatens_i_wi

[78] U.S. Department of Justice, Bureau of Justice Statistics, "Firearm Violence, 1993–2011", May 2013, https://www.bjs.gov/content/pub/pdf/fv9311.pdf.

[79] Ibid.

[80] Ibid.

[81] Insurance Institute for Highway Safety, Highway Loss Data Institute, http://www.iihs.org/iihs/topics/t/general-statistics/fatalityfacts/overview-of-fatality-facts

[82] "Human Errors Drive Growing Death Toll in Auto Crashes," NPR, October 20, 2016, https://www.npr.org/2016/10/20/498406570/tech-human-errors-drive-growing-death-toll-in-auto-crashes

[83] Centers for Disease Control, Priorities for Research to Reduce the Threat of Firearm-Related Violence 2013, https://www.nap.edu/read/18319/chapter/3#15

[84] Gary Kleck and Marc Gertz, "Armed Resistance to Crime: The Prevalence and Nature of Self-Defense with a Gun," *Journal of Criminal Law and Criminology* 150 (1995–1996), https://scholarlycommons.law.northwestern.edu/cgi/viewcontent.cgi?referer=&httpsredir=1&article=6853&context=jclc.

[85] Brian Doherty, "CDC, in Surveys It Never Bothered Making Public, Provides More Evidence That Plenty of Americans Innocently Defend Themselves with Guns," *Reason*, April 20, 2018, https://reason.com/blog/2018/04/20/cdc-provides-more-evidence-that-plenty-o.

[86] Hayden Ludwig, "Why Is the CDC Hiding Its Defensive Gun Use Statistics?" Capital Research Center, April 26, 2018, https://capitalresearch.org/article/why-is-the-cdc-hiding-its-defensive-gun-use-statistics/.

[87] Ibid.

[88] Ibid.

[89] Ibid; Brian Doherty, "CDC, in Surveys It Never Bothered Making Public, Provides More Evidence That Plenty of Americans Innocently Defend Themselves with Guns," *Reason*, April 20, 2018, https://reason.com/blog/2018/04/20/cdc-provides-more-evidence-that-plenty-o.

[90] Hayden Ludwig, "Why Is the CDC Hiding Its Defensive Gun Use Statistics?" Capital Research Center, April 26, 2018, https://capitalresearch.org/article/why-is-the-cdc-hiding-its-defensive-gun-use-statistics/.

[91] "Grandmother Shoots Intruder," WTVY, August 31, 2010, http://www.wtvy.com/home/headlines/101882973.html

[92] "Bridgeport Police: Restaurant Owner Shoots, Kills Armed Robber," *Hartford Courant*, September 27, 2010, http://articles.courant.com/2010–09–27/news/hc-bridgeport-restaurant-shooting-09220100927_1_armed-robber-restaurant-shot-bridgeport-police

[93] "Video: Man killed in attempted robbery in Bessemer linked to others, officials say," *Advance Local*, November 13, 2009, http://blog.al.com/spotnews/2009/11/man_killed_in_attempted_robber.html

[94] FBI, "2016 Crime Statistics Released," September 25, 2017, https://www.fbi.gov/news/stories/2016-crime-statistics-released

[95] Barack Obama, Twitter, February 22, 2013, https://mobile.twitter.com/barackobama/status/304979538927046656?lang=en; President Barack Obama, Weekly Address, January 19, 2013, https://www.youtube.com/watch?v=EJVRgJ8bu0g.

[96] FBI, "Active Shooter Incidents in the United States in 2016 and 2017," https://www.fbi.gov/file-repository/active-shooter-incidents-us-2016-2017.pdf/view

[97] Ibid.

[98] Ibid.

[99] Ibid.

[100] Ibid.

[101] Ibid.

[102] Ibid.

[103] Ibid.

[104] Ibid.

[105] Ibid.

[106] Ibid.

[107] Ibid.

[108] Ibid.

[109] Ibid.

[110] "Officer shoots armed student at high school, charges filed," WRAL, May 16, 2018, https://www.wral.com/officer-shoots-gunman-at-northern-illinois-high-school/17558259/

[111] Ibid.

[112] Ann Coulter, "The Doomsday Scenario: What If School Walkouts Don't Work?" May 23, 2018, *Townhall*, https://townhall.com/columnists/anncoulter/2018/05/23/the-doomsday-scenario-what-if-school-walkouts-dont-work-n2483842

[113] "Churchgoers subdue gunman at Spartanburg church," March 25, 2012, Fox Carolina News, http://www.foxcarolina.com/story/17251517/churchgoers-subdue-gunman-at-spartanburg-church

[114] "'Good Samaritan' Kills Active Shooter in Texas Sports Bar: Police," NBC News, May 4, 2017, https://www.nbcnews.com/news/us-news/good-samaritan-kills-active-shooter-texas-sports-bar-police-n755136

[115] "Deputies: Man opens fire in S.C. bar, draws return fire," Fox 5 News, June 30, 2016, http://www.fox5atlanta.com/news/deputies-man-opens-fire-in-sc-bar-draws-return-fire

[116] "Customer who returned fire at Rockdale County murder suspect called 'hero,'" *Rockdale and Newton Citizen*, May 31, 2015, http://www.rockdalenewtoncitizen.com/news/customer-who-returned-fire-at-rockdale-county-murder-suspect-called/article_4ee4f1bf-8f25-5969-8360-0b9eb21e6c98.html

[117] "Psych patient shoots two at Darby hospital, doctor returns fire," *The Philadelphia Inquirer*, July 24, 2014, http://www.philly.com/philly/news/breaking/20140725_Reports__Three_shot_at_Darby_hospital.html

[118] "Mystic club shooting: Bouncer wondered 'Is this real?' when bullets started flying," *The Oregonian*, January 31, 2014,

http://www.oregonlive.com/portland/index.ssf/2014/01/post _414.html

119 "Waffle House Shooting: 4 Dead in Antioch Shooting," *The Tennessean*, April 22, 2018, https://www.tennessean.com/story/news/2018/04/22/antioch -tn-waffle-house-shooting-naked-suspect/540033002/; "Waffle House Armed Robbery Suspect Hospitalized with Gunshot Wounds: NOPD," *New Orleans Times-Picayune*, April 20, 2018, http://www.nola.com/crime/index.ssf/2018/04/waffle_house _armed_robbery_sus.html.

120 Centers for Disease Control, Priorities for Research to Reduce the Threat of Firearm-Related Violence 2013, https://www.nap.edu/read/18319/chapter/3#15

121 Milton Friedman, "Four Different Ways to Spend Money," June 30, 2010, https://www.financialsamurai.com/the-four-different-ways-to-spend-money-by-milton-friedman/

122 History Channel, Mohandas Ghandi, https://www.history.com/topics/mahatma-gandhi

123 "Texas emergency operator jailed for hanging up on 'thousands' of 911 calls" *The Independent*, April 19, 2018, https://www.independent.co.uk/news/world/americas/texas-911-calls-emergency-hanging-up-jailed-crenshanda-williams-houston-harris-county-a8312726.html

124 "Disgraced Parkland deputy heard shots inside school building, told cops to stay away," *Miami Herald*, March 8, 2018, updated April 17, 2018, http://www.miamiherald.com/news/local/community/broward/article204226584.html

125 Ibid.

126 Ibid.

127 "Stoneman Douglas cop resigns; sheriff says he should have 'killed the killer,'" *Sun Sentinal*, February 23, 2018, http://www.sun-sentinel.com/local/broward/parkland

/florida-school-shooting/fl-florida-shooting-sro-20180222-story.html

[128] "Broward schools' 'culture of leniency' may have been too easy on Nikolas Cruz, report finds," Fox News, May 13, 2018, http://www.foxnews.com/us/2018/05/13/broward-schools-culture-leniency-may-have-been-too-easy-on-nikolas-cruz-report-finds.html

[129] "Columbine High School Shootings Fast Facts," CNN, March 25, 2018, https://www.cnn.com/2013/09/18/us/columbine-high-school-shootings-fast-facts/index.html

[130] Ibid.

[131] *Rampage: Spree Killers and Mass Murderers*, RJ Parker, RJ Parker Publishing, 2012, p. 80-81, https://books.google.com/books?id=F53ZBQAAQBAJ&pg=PA80&lpg=PA80&dq=Jefferson+County+Sheriff%E2%80%99s+investigator+Michael+Guerra+also+discovered+a+variety+of+threats+against+Columbine+teachers+and+students&source=bl&ots=XXyTOaFdlQ&sig=GkshlVj6sGoxBlDFbMhMN_MyBCY&hl=en&sa=X&ved=0ahUKEwiOiMWHlpjbAhVh64MKHUacBu0Q6AEIWDAH#v=onepage&q=Jefferson%20County%20Sheriff%E2%80%99s%20investigator%20Michael%20Guerra%20also%20discovered%20a%20variety%20of%20threats%20against%20Columbine%20teachers%20and%20students&f=false

[132] *Rampage: Spree Killers and Mass Murderers*, RJ Parker, RJ Parker Publishing, 2012, p. 80, https://books.google.com/books?id=F53ZBQAAQBAJ&pg=PA80&lpg=PA80&dq=Jefferson+County+Sheriff%E2%80%99s+investigator+Michael+Guerra+also+discovered+a+variety+of+threats+against+Columbine+teachers+and+students&source=bl&ots=XXyTOaFdlQ&sig=GkshlVj6sGoxBlDFbMhMN_MyBCY&hl=en&sa=X&ved=0ahUKEwiOiMWHlpjbAhVh64MKHUacBu0Q6AEIWDAH#v=onepage&q=Jefferson%20County%20Sheriff%E2%80%99s%20investigator%20Michael%20Guerra%20also%20discovered%20a%20variety%20of%20threats%20against%20Columbine%20teachers%20and%20students&f=false

[133] Ibid, 80-81.

[134] Ibid.

[135] Ibid.

[136] Ibid.

[137] "Everything we know about the San Bernardino terror attack investigation so far," *Los Angeles Times*, December 14, 2015, http://www.latimes.com/local/california/la-me-san-bernardino-shooting-terror-investigation-htmlstory.html

[138] Ibid.

[139] Ibid.

[140] "San Bernardino shooting: Couple radicalized before they met, FBI says," CNN, December 9, 2015, https://www.cnn.com/2015/12/09/us/san-bernardino-shooting/index.html

[141] Ibid.

[142] Ibid.

[143] "Lessons Learned from the Police Response to the San Bernardino and Orlando Terrorist Attacks," Combating Terrorism Center at West Point, May 2017, v.10, issue 5, https://ctc.usma.edu/lessons-learned-from-the-police-response-to-the-san-bernardino-and-orlando-terrorist-attacks/

[144] Ibid.

[145] Ibid.

[146] "One year after the San Bernardino attack, police offer a possible motive as questions still linger," *The Washington Post*, December 2, 2016, https://www.washingtonpost.com/news/post-nation/wp/2016/12/02/one-year-after-san-bernardino-police-offer-a-possible-motive-as-questions-still-linger/?utm_term=.1d27b6b6e7c1

[147] "The FBI investigated the Orlando mass shooter for 10 months — and found nothing. Here's why," *Los Angeles Times*, Jul 14, 2016, http://www.latimes.com/nation/la-na-fbi-investigation-mateen-20160712-snap-story.html

[148] "3 Hours In Orlando: Piecing Together An Attack And Its Aftermath," NPR, June 26, 2016, https://www.npr.org/2016/06/16/482322488/orlando-shooting-what-happened-update

[149] "Orlando shooting: What motivated a killer?," CNN, June 14, 2016, https://www.cnn.com/2016/06/13/us/orlando-nightclub-shooting/index.html; "Lessons Learned from the Police Response to the San Bernardino and Orlando Terrorist Attacks," Combating Terrorism Center at West Point, May 2017, v.10, issue 5, https://ctc.usma.edu/lessons-learned-from-the-police-response-to-the-san-bernardino-and-orlando-terrorist-attacks/

[150] "Police tactics expert rips Orlando SWAT team that waited to breach Pulse nightclub during horrific mass shooting," *New York Daily News*, June 13, 2016, http://www.nydailynews.com/news/national/police-tactics-expert-rips-orlando-response-club-shooting-article-1.2671907

[151] "'They took too damn long': Inside the police response to the Orlando Shooting," *The Washington Post*, August 1, 2016, https://www.washingtonpost.com/world/national-security/they-took-too-damn-long-inside-the-police-response-to-the-orlando-shooting/2016/08/01/67a66130-5447-11e6-88eb-7dda4e2f2aec_story.html?noredirect=on&utm_term=.3185a3f838a1

[152] Ibid.

[153] "First responders recognized for Pulse nightclub attack response," WFTV9 ABC, May 4, 2017, https://www.wftv.com/news/local/first-responders-recognized-for-pulse-nightclub-attack-response/519310270

[154] "From 'shots fired' to all clear: 72 minutes of terror in Las Vegas," *Los Angeles Times*, Oct. 3, 2017, http://www.latimes.com/projects/la-na-las-vegas-response/

[155] Ibid.

[156] "Galveston Sheriff: Officers Engaged With Santa Fe Shooter in 4 Minutes," NBCDFW 5, May 21, 2018, https://www.nbcdfw.com/news/local/Santa-Fe-School-Shooting-Police-Response-483196531.html

[157] "Police Confronted Santa Fe School Shooting Suspect Within 4 Minutes and Exchanged Gunfire With Him," *TIME*, May 22, 2018, http://time.com/5286856/santa-fe-shooting-victims-police-crossfire/

[158] Ibid.

[159] "Sandy Hook shooting: What happened?," CNN, December 2012, http://www.cnn.com/interactive/2012/12/us/sandy-hook-timeline/index.html

[160] Ibid.

[161] "When Seconds Count The Police Are Only Two Minutes Away," *The Truth About Guns*, March 11, 2012, http://www.thetruthaboutguns.com/2012/03/robert-farago/when-seconds-count-the-police-are-only-two-minutes-away/

[162] "It's official: Gawker.com has closed," *Business Insider*, August 23, 2016, http://www.businessinsider.com/gawkercom-closes-final-story-hulk-hogan-peter-thiel-nick-denton-2016-8

[163] Don B. Kates, Jr., GUNS, MURDERS, AND THE CONSTITUTION, A Realistic Assessment of Gun Control, 1990, https://www.azcdl.org/Kates_GunsMurdersandtheConstitution.pdf, p. 19

[164] "Racial justice groups are sending thousands of black and brown kids to the March for Our Lives rally," *Mic*, March 23, 2018, https://mic.com/articles/188560/racial-justice-groups-are-

sending-thousands-of-black-and-brown-kids-to-the-march-for-our-lives-rally#.BUPpCsFrW

[165] Black Lives Matter Campaign Zero, https://www.joincampaignzero.org/solutions/#brokenwindows

[166] Ibid.

[167] Ibid.

[168] Heritage Foundation Backgrounder, "Focusing on School Safety After Parkland," March 19, 2018, https://www.heritage.org/sites/default/files/2018-03/BG3295.pdf; Grant Duwe, "The Patterns and Prevalence of Mass Public Shootings in the United States, 1915–2013" https://www.hoplofobia.info/wp-content/uploads/2015/08/The-Patterns-and-Prevalence-of-Mass-Public-Shootings.pdf

[169] "Adam Lanza's Mental Problems 'Completely Untreated' Before Newtown Shootings, Report Says," *The New York Times*, November 21, 2014, https://www.nytimes.com/2014/11/22/nyregion/before-newtown-shootings-adam-lanzas-mental-problems-completely-untreated-report-says.html

[170] Ibid.

[171] Ibid.

[172] "Sandy Hook shooting: What happened?" CNN, December 2012, http://www.cnn.com/interactive/2012/12/us/sandy-hook-timeline/index.html

[173] "Red flags: The troubled path of accused Parkland shooter Nikolas Cruz," *The Washington Post*, March 10, 2018, https://www.washingtonpost.com/graphics/2018/national/timeline-parkland-shooter-nikolas-cruz/

[174] Ibid.

[175] Ibid.

[176] Ibid.

[177] Ibid.

[178] "Police identify Calif. shooting suspect as Elliot Rodger," *USA Today*, May 24, 2014, https://www.usatoday.com/story/news/usanow/2014/05/24/shooting-california-santa-barbara/9532405/

[179] "Peter Rodger: Elliot was not evil, but he was mentally ill," *Los Angeles Times*, June 27, 2014, http://www.latimes.com/local/lanow/la-me-peter-rodger-son-20140627-story.html

[180] "Elliot Rodger Report Details Long Struggle with Mental Illness," *Santa Barbara Independent*, February 20, 2015, https://www.independent.com/news/2015/feb/20/elliot-rodger-report-details-long-struggle-mental-/

[181] "A look inside the 'broken' mind of James Holmes," CNN, June 10, 2015, https://www.cnn.com/2015/06/05/us/james-holmes-theater-shooting-trial/index.html

[182] Ibid.

[183] "Doctor who found James Holmes sane says mental illness caused him to attack Colorado theater," Fox News, July 27, 2015, http://www.foxnews.com/us/2015/07/27/doctor-who-found-james-holmes-sane-says-mental-illness-caused-him-to-attack.html

[184] Ibid.

[185] Ibid.

[186] "POSSESSION OF FIREARMS BY PEOPLE WITH MENTAL ILLNESS," National Conference of State Legislatures, January 5, 2018, http://www.ncsl.org/research/civil-and-criminal-justice/possession-of-a-firearm-by-the-mentally-ill.aspx

[187] Ibid.

[188] "Half of all Americans now live in 'sanctuaries' protecting immigrants," *The Washington Times*, May 10, 2018, https://www.washingtontimes.com/news/2018/may/10/half-of-americans-now-live-in-sanctuaries/

[189] "The Current Gun Debate: Mass Shootings," *The Heritage Foundation*, March 12, 2018, https://www.heritage.org/the-constitution/report/the-current-gun-debate-mass-shootings.

[190] Ibid.

[191] "Suspect In October New York Truck Attack Pleads Not Guilty," NPR, November 29, 2017, https://www.npr.org/sections/thetwo-way/2017/11/29/567125421/suspect-in-october-new-york-truck-attack-pleads-not-guilty

[192] The History Channel, OKLAHOMA CITY BOMBING, https://www.history.com/topics/oklahoma-city-bombing

[193] "Arsonist who torched 87 people in horrific 1990 Happy Land fire dies after apparent heart attack in prison," *New York Daily News*, September 13, 2016, http://www.nydailynews.com/new-york/arsonist-torched-87-people-happy-land-club-died-prison-article-1.2791168

[194] "David Burke's Deadly Revenge," *TIME*, June 24, 2001, http://content.time.com/time/magazine/article/0,9171,145653,00.html

[195] "Before Orlando: The (former) deadliest LGBT attack in U.S. history," CNN, June 19, 2016, https://www.cnn.com/2016/06/16/health/1973-new-orleans-gay-bar-arson-attack/index.html; "Remembering The UpStairs Lounge Fire That Killed 32 LGBTQ People," *The Huffington Post*, June 24, 2017, https://www.huffingtonpost.com/entry/upstairs-lounge-fire_us_5947160ce4b06bb7d2741b3a

[196] "Germanwings Flight 9525 co-pilot deliberately crashed plane, officials say," CNN, March 26, 2015, https://www.cnn.com/2015/03/26/europe/france-germanwings-plane-crash-main/index.html

[197] World Economic Forum Travel and Tourism Competitiveness Report 2017, http://reports.weforum.org/travel-and-tourism-competitiveness-report-2017/ranking/#series=TTCI.A.02

198 "These were the 50 most violent cities in the world in 2017," *Business Insider*, March 6, 2018, http://www.businessinsider.com/most-violent-cities-in-the-world-2018-3

199 FBI, Crime in the U.S. 2016, https://ucr.fbi.gov/crime-in-the-u.s/2016/crime-in-the-u.s.-2016/tables/table-12

200 "London murder rate overtakes New York's," BBC News, April 2, 2018, http://www.bbc.com/news/uk-england-london-43610936

201 "Police chiefs to discuss offering guns to all frontline officers," *The Guardian*, June 23, 2017, https://www.theguardian.com/uk-news/2017/jun/23/police-chiefs-to-discuss-offering-guns-to-all-frontline-officers

202 "London attack: Seven killed in vehicle and stabbing incidents," BBC News, June 4, 2017, http://www.bbc.com/news/uk-40146916; "London attack: 12 arrested in Barking after van and knife attack," BBC, June 5, 2017, http://www.bbc.com/news/uk-40148737

203 Ibid.

204 Ibid.

205 "Knife-wielding attackers kill 29, injure 130 at China train station," CNN, March 2, 2014, https://www.cnn.com/2014/03/01/world/asia/china-railway-attack/index.html

206 "Nine school children killed in China knife attack blamed on angry former pupil," *South China Morning Post*, April 28, 2018, http://www.scmp.com/news/china/policies-politics/article/2143776/seven-schoolchildren-killed-china-knife-attack-blamed

207 Every Town for Gun Safety, https://everytownresearch.org/

208 Ibid.

209 Association for Safe International Road Travel, http://asirt.org/initiatives/informing-road-users/road-safety-facts/road-crash-statistics

[210] "Guns kill nearly 1,300 US children each year, study says," CNN, June 19, 2017, https://www.cnn.com/2017/06/19/health/child-gun-violence-study/index.html

[211] Centers for Disease Control, National Center for Health Statistics, Fast Stats, https://www.cdc.gov/nchs/fastats/injury.htm

[212] Centers for Disease Control, National Center for Health Statistics, Homicide Mortality by State, https://www.cdc.gov/nchs/pressroom/sosmap/homicide_mortality/homicide.htm

[213] Statistica Canada, Homicide in Canada, 2016, November 22, 2017, http://www.statcan.gc.ca/pub/85-002-x/2017001/article/54879-eng.htm; Knoema, World Data Atlas, Belgium Homicide Rate, 2015, https://knoema.com/atlas/Belgium/Homicide-rate; Office of National Statistics, Homicide in England and Wales, year ending March 2017, https://www.ons.gov.uk/peoplepopulationandcommunity/crimeandjustice/articles/homicideinenglandandwales/yearendingmarch2017; "Australia's murder rate falls to record low of one person per 100,000," *The Guardian*, June 18, 2017, https://www.theguardian.com/australia-news/2017/jun/18/australias-rate-falls-to-record-low-of-one-person-per-100000

[214] "Chicago's 762 homicides in 2016 is highest in 19 years," CNN, January 2, 2017, https://www.cnn.com/2017/01/01/us/chicago-murders-2016/index.html

[215] "Vermont ranks No. 1 on safest states list," *Burlington Free Press*, November 14, 2016, https://www.burlingtonfreepress.com/story/news/2016/11/14/vt-ranks-no-1-safest-states-list/93799588/

[216] Centers for Disease Control, Homicide Mortality by State 2016, https://www.cdc.gov/nchs/pressroom/sosmap/homicide_mortality/homicide.htm

[217] The Heritage Foundation, Gun Control Fact Sheet, March 12, 2018, https://www.heritage.org/sites/default/files/2018-03/Gun%20Violence_1.pdf

[218] "These States Have the Most Restrictive Gun Laws in America," *CheatSheet*, May 20, 2018, https://www.cheatsheet.com/culture/these-states-have-the-most-restrictive-gun-laws-in-america.html/?a=viewall

[219] "Murders in US very concentrated: 54% of US counties in 2014 had zero murders, 2% of counties have 51% of the murders," Crime Prevention Research Center, April 25, 2017, https://crimeresearch.org/2017/04/number-murders-county-54-us-counties-2014-zero-murders-69-1-murder/

[220] Ibid.

[221] Ibid.

[222] Ibid.

[223] Ibid.

[224] "Murder rates drop as concealed carry permits soar: report," *The Washington Times*, July 14, 2015, https://www.washingtontimes.com/news/2015/jul/14/murder-rates-drop-as-concealed-carry-permits-soar-/

[225] "Immigration to the United States after 1945," American History, Oxford Research Encyclopedias, July 2016, http://americanhistory.oxfordre.com/view/10.1093/acrefore/9780199329175.001.0001/acrefore-9780199329175-e-72

[226] United Nations, https://dataunodc.un.org/crime/intentional-homicide-victims (accessed June 11, 2018)

[227] "The Media Bubble Is Worse Than You Think," *Politico*, May/June 2017, https://www.politico.com/magazine/story/2017/04/25/media-bubble-real-journalism-jobs-east-coast-215048

[228] Ibid.

[229] "Is the New York Times a Liberal Newspaper?" *The New York Times*, July 25, 2004,

https://www.nytimes.com/2004/07/25/opinion/the-public-editor-is-the-new-york-times-a-liberal-newspaper.html

230 "The bias against guns: What the media isn't telling you," Fox News, January 9, 2015, http://www.foxnews.com/opinion/2015/01/09/bias-against-guns-what-media-isnt-telling.html

231 Parkland Generated Dramatically More News Coverage Than Most Mass Shootings, *The Trace*, May 17, 2018, https://www.thetrace.org/2018/05/parkland-media-coverage-analysis-mass-shooting/

232 "UPDATE: James Shaw Jr. raises $227,000 for Waffle House shooting victims," WHIO, April 27, 2018, https://www.whio.com/news/james-shaw-raises-165–000-for-waffle-house-shooting-victims/3XRBrqrfwDvRXtJiGw4noN/

233 "Waffle House armed robbery suspect hospitalized with gunshot wounds: NOPD," *Times-Picayune*, April 20, 2018, http://www.nola.com/crime/index.ssf/2018/04/waffle_house_armed_robbery_sus.html

234 "Waffle House hero James Shaw Jr. meets with Parkland shooting survivors," *New York Daily News*, May 13, 2018, http://www.nydailynews.com/news/national/waffle-house-hero-james-shaw-jr-meets-parkland-survivors-article-1.3987355

235 Greg Myre, "A Brief History Of The AR-15," NPR, February 28, 2018, https://www.npr.org/2018/02/28/588861820/a-brief-history-of-the-ar-15

236 Ibid.

237 Justin Carissimo, "26 Dead in Shooting at Church in Sutherland Springs, Texas," CBS News, November 6, 2017, https://www.cbsnews.com/news/texas-church-shooting-devin-patrick-kelley-first-baptist-church-sutherland-springs-live-updates/; "Man Who Opened Fire on Sutherland Springs Shooter Honored at NRA Convention," CBS News, May 4, 2018, https://www.cbsnews.com/news/stephen-

willeford-sutherland-springs-nra-convention-today-2018-05-04/

[238] "AR-15-Wielding Neighbor Speaks Out, 2 Charged In Stabbing," *Patch*, February 27, 2018, https://patch.com/illinois/oswego/ar-15-threat-used-stop-knife-attack-sheriff

[239] "AR-15 Used for North Carolina Home Defense," *The Truth About Guns*, February 13, 2018, http://www.thetruthaboutguns.com/2018/02/dean-weingarten/ar-15-used-for-north-carolina-home-defense/

[240] "Defensive Use of AR-15, Man Kills Two, Wounds One Attacker," *Ammoland*, September 15, 2017, https://www.ammoland.com/2017/09/defensive-use-of-ar-15-man-kills-two-wounds-one-of-three-attackers/

[241] "Homeowner's son kills three would-be burglars with AR-15," *New York Post*, March 28, 2017, https://nypost.com/2017/03/28/homeowners-son-kills-three-would-be-burglars-with-ar-15/

[242] "In Ferguson, black residents stand guard at white-owned store," Reuters, November 26, 2014, https://www.reuters.com/article/us-usa-missouri-shooting-gasstation/in-ferguson-black-residents-stand-guard-at-white-owned-store-idUSKCN0JA1XF20141126

[243] John Hayward, ""Assault rifle" saves teenagers from home invasion burglars," *Human Events*, January 10, 2013, http://humanevents.com/2013/01/10/assault-rifle-saves-teenagers-from-home-invasion-burglars/

[244] "No Shots Fired: Home Intruders Decide Not to Stick Around After Seeing Their 'Victim' Holding an AR-15," *The Blaze*, January 24, 2013, https://www.theblaze.com/stories/2013/01/24/no-shots-fired-home-intruders-decide-not-to-stick-around-after-seeing-their-victim-holding-an-ar-15

[245] AWR Hawkins, "Who Needs an AR-15?" *Breitbart*, January 14, 2013, http://www.breitbart.com/big-government/2013/01/14/who-needs-an-ar-15/.

[246] FBI, Crime in the United States 2016, https://ucr.fbi.gov/crime-in-the-u.s/2016/crime-in-the-u.s.-2016/tables/table-12

[247] Ibid.

[248] Benny Johnson, "According to the FBI, Knives Kill Far More People Than Rifles in America—It's Not Even Close," *The Daily Caller*, February 19, 2018, http://dailycaller.com/2018/02/19/knives-gun-control-fbi-statistics/; FBI, "Crime in the United States, 2016," https://ucr.fbi.gov/crime-in-the-u.s/2016/crime-in-the-u.s.-2016/tables/table-12.

[249] Emily Larsen, "Fact Check: Are Most Gun Crimes Committed with Handguns?" *Daily Signal*, February 22, 2018, https://www.dailysignal.com/2018/02/22/fact-check-are-most-gun-crimes-committed-with-handguns/.

[250] "Can Mass Shootings be Stopped," Rockefeller Institute of Government, May 22, 2018, http://rockinst.org/issue-area/can-mass-shootings-be-stopped/

[251] Erik Larson, "Federal Judge Upholds Massachusetts's Assault-Weapons Ban," *Bloomberg*, April 6, 2018, https://www.bloomberg.com/news/articles/2018-04-06/massachusetts-s-ban-on-assault-weapons-upheld-by-federal-judge

[252] Brent McCluskey, "The History of Magazines Holding 11 or More Rounds: A Response to California's Magazine Ban," *Guns.com*, June 3, 2014, http://www.guns.com/2014/06/03/the-history-of-magazines-holding-11-or-more-rounds-a-response-to-californias-magazine-ban/.

[253] "Before Gatling – Who Was The First To Invent A Rapid-Fire Gun?" *Military History Now*, January 27, 2014, https://militaryhistorynow.com/2014/01/27/before-gatling-who-was-the-first-to-invent-the-rapid-fire-gun/

[254] Eli Whitney Museum and Workshop, The Factory, https://www.eliwhitney.org/7/museum/about-eli-whitney/factory

255 The Franklin Institute, Benjamin Franklin's Inventions, https://www.fi.edu/benjamin-franklin/inventions

256 Joe Kissell, "The Inventions of Thomas Jefferson" Interesting Things of the Day, April 20, 2018, https://itotd.com/articles/2385/the-inventions-of-thomas-jefferson/

257 ConstitutionFacts.com, Inventions of the Founding Fathers, https://www.constitutionfacts.com/founders-library/founding-fathers-inventions/

258 "High-Capacity Gun Magazine Bans: The Numbers, the Opposing Arguments, the Unexpected Origin Story," *The Trace*, July 29, 2015, https://www.thetrace.org/2015/07/magazine-capacity-limit-explainer/

259 Giffords Law Center to Prevent Gun Violence. http://lawcenter.giffords.org/gun-laws/policy-areas/hardware-ammunition/large-capacity-magazines/

260 Ibid.

261 H.R.3355 - Violent Crime Control and Law Enforcement Act of 1994, Congress.gov, https://www.congress.gov/bill/103rd-congress/house-bill/3355/text

262 "Study: Gun-Related Murder Rates Higher Under 'Assault Weapons' Ban," *Breitbart*, April 7, 2014, http://www.breitbart.com/big-government/2014/04/07/study-gun-related-murder-rates-19-3-percent-higher-under-assault-weapons-ban/

263 Mission Statement, March for Our Lives, https://marchforourlives.com/mission-statement/

264 "Report: Parkland Shooter Did Not Use High-Capacity Magazines," *National Review*, March 1, 2018, https://www.nationalreview.com/2018/03/report-parkland-shooter-did-not-use-high-capacity-magazines/

265 "Alleged shooter at Texas high school spared people he liked, court document says," CNN, May 19, 2018,

https://www.cnn.com/2018/05/18/us/texas-school-shooting/index.html

266 "Virginia Tech Shootings Fast Facts" CNN, May 2, 2018, https://www.cnn.com/2013/10/31/us/virginia-tech-shootings-fast-facts/index.html

267 "Nice attack: What we know about the Bastille Day killings," BBC News, August 19, 2016, http://www.bbc.com/news/world-europe-36801671

268 "All 10 victims of the Toronto van attack have been identified," CNN, April 27, 2018, https://www.cnn.com/2018/04/27/americas/toronto-van-attack-victims-list-toronto/index.html

269 "Columbine High School Shootings Fast Facts," CNN, March 25, 2018, https://www.cnn.com/2013/09/18/us/columbine-high-school-shootings-fast-facts/index.html

270 "San Bernardino shooting: Couple radicalized before they met, FBI says," CNN, December 9, 2015, https://www.cnn.com/2015/12/09/us/san-bernardino-shooting/index.html

271 "September 11th Hijackers Fast Facts," CNN, August 28, 2017, https://www.cnn.com/2013/07/27/us/september-11th-hijackers-fast-facts/index.html

272 "What happened at the Bataclan?" BBC News, December 9, 2015, http://www.bbc.com/news/world-europe-34827497

273 "UPDATED: Mass Public Shootings keep occurring in Gun-Free Zones: 97.3% of attacks since 1950" Crime Prevention Research Center, May 19, 2018, https://crimeresearch.org/2018/05/more-misleading-information-from-bloombergs-everytown-for-gun-safety-on-guns-analysis-of-recent-mass-shootings/

274 "17 killed in mass shooting at high school in Parkland, Florida," NBC News, February 15, 2018, https://www.nbcnews.com/news/us-news/police-respond-shooting-parkland-florida-high-school-n848101

275 "Nine victims and gunman dead in mass shooting at Ore. community college," *The Washington Post*, October 2, 2015, https://www.washingtonpost.com/national/multiple-fatalities-reported-in-shooting-at-oregon-community-college/2015/10/01/b9e9cc4c-686c-11e5-9ef3-fde182507eac_story.html

276 "27 dead in Newtown, CT., elementary school shooting," MSNBC, December 14, 2012, http://www.msnbc.com/msnbc/27-dead-newtown-ct-elementary-school-s

277 "Virginia Tech Shootings Fast Facts," CNN, May 2, 2018, https://www.cnn.com/2013/10/31/us/virginia-tech-shootings-fast-facts/index.html

278 "Columbine High School Shootings Fast Facts," CNN, March 25, 2018, https://www.cnn.com/2013/09/18/us/columbine-high-school-shootings-fast-facts/index.html

279 "At least 14 people killed in shooting in San Bernardino; suspect identified," CNN, December 3, 2015, https://www.cnn.com/2015/12/02/us/san-bernardino-shooting/index.html

280 "Army major kills 13 people in Fort Hood shooting spree," *History*, https://www.history.com/this-day-in-history/army-major-kills-13-people-in-fort-hood-shooting-spree

281 "4 dead, including shooter, at Fort Hood," CNN, April 3, 2014, https://www.cnn.com/2014/04/02/us/fort-hood-shooting/index.html

282 "UPDATED: Mass Public Shootings keep occurring in Gun-Free Zones: 97.3% of attacks since 1950," Crime Prevention Research Center, May 9, 2018, https://crimeresearch.org/2018/05/more-misleading-information-from-bloombergs-everytown-for-gun-safety-on-guns-analysis-of-recent-mass-shootings/

283 Ibid.

284 Ibid.

285 Ibid.

[286] Ibid.

[287] Ibid.

[288] Ibid.

[289] Ibid.

[290] Ibid.

[291] "Another Shooting in a Gun-free Zone: Nine Dead at the Emanuel African Methodist Episcopal Church in Charleston, South Carolina," Crime Prevention Research Center, June 18, 2015, https://crimeresearch.org/2015/06/another-shooting-in-a-gun-free-zone-nine-dead-at-the-charleston-african-american-church/

[292] Ibid.

[293] Ibid.

[294] "Police release photos from Accent Signage mass killing," *Star Tribune*, June 6, 2013, http://www.startribune.com/police-release-photos-from-accent-signage-mass-killing/210395321/

[295] "UPDATED: Mass Public Shootings keep occurring in Gun-Free Zones: 97.3% of attacks since 1950," Crime Prevention Research Center, May 9, 2018, https://crimeresearch.org/2018/05/more-misleading-information-from-bloombergs-everytown-for-gun-safety-on-guns-analysis-of-recent-mass-shootings/

[296] "Police release photos from Accent Signage mass killing," *Star Tribune*, June 6, 2013, http://www.startribune.com/police-release-photos-from-accent-signage-mass-killing/210395321/

[297] John R. Lott, "Did Colorado shooter single out Cinemark theater because it banned guns?" FoxNews, September 10, 2012, http://www.foxnews.com/opinion/2012/09/10/did-colorado-shooter-single-out-cinemark-theater.html

[298] "No guns policy at Cinemark Theaters?" John Lott's Website, July 20, 2012, http://johnrlott.blogspot.com/2012/07/no-guns-policy-at-cinemark-theaters.html

[299] John R. Lott, "Did Colorado shooter single out Cinemark theater because it banned guns?" FoxNews, September 10, 2012, http://www.foxnews.com/opinion/2012/09/10/did-colorado-shooter-single-out-cinemark-theater.html

[300] "Politifact's continued biased and flawed evaluations about gun control: France had a higher casualty rate in one year than the entire 8 years of Barack Obama," Crime Prevention Research Center, March 12, 2018, https://crimeresearch.org/2018/03/politifacts-continued-biased-flawed-evaluations-gun-control-france-higher-casualty-rate-one-year-entire-8-years-barack-obama/

[301] "Repeal gun-free zones," USA Today, February 15, 2018, https://www.usatoday.com/story/opinion/2018/02/15/repeal-gun-free-zones-erich-pratt-editorials-debates/110464412/

[302] "UPDATED: Comparing Death Rates from Mass Public Shootings and Mass Public Violence in the US and Europe," Crime Prevention Research Center, June 23, 2015, https://crimeresearch.org/2015/06/comparing-death-rates-from-mass-public-shootings-in-the-us-and-europe/

[303] Ibid.

[304] Ibid.

[305] "New evidence confirms what gun rights advocates have said for a long time about crime," The Washington Post, July 27, 2016, https://www.washingtonpost.com/news/wonk/wp/2016/07/27/new-evidence-confirms-what-gun-rights-advocates-have-been-saying-for-a-long-time-about-crime/?utm_term=.2a7a11ffd696

[306] "Western European countries have some of the strictest gun control laws in the world. How France cut its per capita gun ownership in half," CNN, February 26, 2018, https://www.cnn.com/2018/02/26/opinions/france-america-gun-laws-opinion-andelman/index.html (France); "Gun control and ownership laws in the UK," BBC, November 2,

2010, http://www.bbc.com/news/10220974 (United
Kingdom); Firearms-Control Legislation and Policy: Spain,
https://www.loc.gov/law/help/firearms-
control/spain.php (Spain); Guns in the Republic of Ireland,
http://www.gunpolicy.org/firearms/region/cp/ireland
(Ireland)

[307] "France train attack: Americans overpower gunman on Paris
express" *The Guardian*, August 22, 2015,
https://www.theguardian.com/world/2015/aug/21/amsterda
m-paris-train-gunman-france

[308] "2015 Paris Terror Attacks Fast Facts," CNN, May 2, 2018,
https://www.cnn.com/2015/12/08/europe/2015-paris-terror-
attacks-fast-facts/index.html

[309] "Mexicans have the right to own guns, but few do," CBS News,
August 17, 2016, https://www.cbsnews.com/news/mexicans-
have-the-right-to-own-guns-but-few-do/

[310] "EXCLUSIVE — PHOTOS: Mexican Cartel Improves
Weapons Manufacturing Capabilities," *Breitbart*, February 1,
2018, http://www.breitbart.com/texas/2018/02/01/exclusive-
photos-mexican-cartel-improves-weapons-manufacturing-
capabilities/

[311] Australian Institute of Criminology, Australian Crime Facts
and Figures 2007,
https://www.secasa.com.au/assets/Statstics/australian-crime-
facts-and-figures-2007-.pdf

[312] "Outside the Americas, Knives Are Often the Weapon of
Choice in Homicides," *Smithsonian Magazine*, March 3,
2014, https://www.smithsonianmag.com/smart-
news/outside-americas-knives-are-often-weapon-choice-
homicides-180949953/; "London murder rate overtakes New
York as knife crime rises," Reuters, April 3, 2018
https://www.reuters.com/article/us-britain-crime-
murder/london-murder-rate-overtakes-new-york-as-knife-
crime-rises-idUSKCN1HA1DH; "Paris Attack Leaves 1
Dead and 4 Wounded by Knife-Wielding Terrorist," *The
New York Times*, May 12, 2018,

https://www.nytimes.com/2018/05/12/world/europe/paris-knife-attack-stabbing-france.html

313 "Pressure-cooker bomb used in Chelsea seen in other US attacks," *New York Post*, September 19, 2016, https://nypost.com/2016/09/19/terrorists-still-favor-pressure-cooker-used-in-chelsea-bombing/

314 "A list of attacks involving vans running into people over past years," *National Post*, April 23, 2018, http://nationalpost.com/pmn/news-pmn/canada-news-pmn/a-list-of-attacks-involving-vans-running-into-people-over-past-years

315 "Burning Kites From Gaza Cause Widespread Damage to Israeli Fields," *Haaretz*, May 29, 2018, https://www.haaretz.com/israel-news/.premium.MAGAZINE-burning-kites-from-gaza-cause-widespread-damage-to-israeli-fields-1.6131396

316 "Sweden has a problem with hand grenades — and here's why," *Euronews*, April 10, 2018, http://www.euronews.com/2018/04/10/sweden-has-a-problem-with-hand-grenades-and-here-s-why

317 "Hand Grenades and Gang Violence Rattle Sweden's Middle Class," *The New York Times*, March 3, 2018, https://www.nytimes.com/2018/03/03/world/europe/sweden-crime-immigration-hand-grenades.html?

318 "What Brazil Can Teach America About Gun Control," *Newstalk 1130*, Dan O'Donnell, https://newstalk1130.iheart.com/featured/common-sense-central/content/2018-02-21-what-brazil-can-teach-america-about-gun-control/; "Brazil Has Nearly 60,000 Murders, And It May Relax Gun Laws" NPR, March 28, 2016, https://www.npr.org/sections/parallels/2016/03/28/472157969/brazil-has-nearly-60-000-murders-and-it-may-relax-gun-laws ; "People Are Ready to Buy Some Guns in the World's Murder Capital," *Bloomberg*, March 20, 2018, https://www.bloomberg.com/news/articles/2018-03-20/in-world-s-murder-capital-brazilians-are-ready-to-buy-some-guns

[319] "Guns kill about 40,000 Brazilians every year. Some lawmakers think more guns will make the country safer," *PRI*, March 29, 2017, https://www.pri.org/stories/2017-03-29/guns-kill-about-40000-brazilians-every-year-some-lawmakers-think-more-guns-will

[320] "Brazil Has Nearly 60,000 Murders, And It May Relax Gun Laws," NPR, March 28, 2016, https://www.npr.org/sections/parallels/2016/03/28/4721579 69/brazil-has-nearly-60-000-murders-and-it-may-relax-gun-laws

[321] "People Are Ready to Buy Some Guns in the World's Murder Capital," *Bloomberg*, March 20, 2018, https://www.bloomberg.com/news/articles/2018-03-20/in-world-s-murder-capital-brazilians-are-ready-to-buy-some-guns

[322] Congressional Research Service, Report for Congress, Gun Control Legislation, p. 8, November 14, 2012, https://fas.org/sgp/crs/misc/RL32842.pdf

[323] ATF 2017 Report on Firearms Commerce in the U.S, https://www.atf.gov/news/pr/atf-releases-2017-report-firearms-commerce-us

[324] Ibid.

[325] "GUN SALES DOWN AFTER OBAMA BOOM YEARS," *Newsweek*, March 23, 2017, http://www.newsweek.com/gun-sales-down-after-obama-boom-years-573170

[326] Crime Prevention Research Center, Concealed Carry Permit Holders Across the United States: 2017 by John Lott (July 2017) https://crimeresearch.org/2017/07/new-study-16-3-million-concealed-handgun-permits-last-year-saw-largest-increase-ever-number-permits/

[327] Ibid.

[328] Ibid.

[329] Congressional Research Service, Report for Congress, Gun Control Legislation, p. 9, November 14, 2012, https://fas.org/sgp/crs/misc/RL32842.pdf

[330] "Rate Of U.S. Gun Violence Has Fallen Since 1993, Study Says," NPR, May 7, 2013, https://www.npr.org/sections/thetwo-way/2013/05/07/181998015/rate-of-u-s-gun-violence-has-fallen-since-1993-study-says

[331] Grant Duwe, "The Patterns and Prevalence of Mass Public Shootings in the United States, 1915–2013," https://www.hoplofobia.info/wp-content/uploads/2015/08/The-Patterns-and-Prevalence-of-Mass-Public-Shootings.pdf

[332] "No Child Left Alone: Moral Judgments about Parents Affect Estimates of Risk to Children," University of California Press, https://www.collabra.org/article/10.1525/collabra.33/; "Availability: A heuristic for judging frequency and probability," *Science Direct, Cognitive Psychology,* vol 5 issue 2, September 1973, https://www.sciencedirect.com/science/article/pii/0010028573900339?via%3Dihub

[333] Graham C. L. Davey, The Psychological Effects of TV News, *Psychology Today,* June 19, 2012, https://www.psychologytoday.com/intl/blog/why-we-worry/201206/the-psychological-effects-tv-news?amp=

[334] "Exploiting Orlando: Nets Advance Anti-Gun Agenda By 8 to 1," Media Research Center, June 22, 2016, https://www.newsbusters.org/blogs/nb/2016/06/22/exploiting-orlando-nets-advance-anti-gun-agenda-8-1

[335] Ibid.

[336] Ibid.

[337] "Despite Heightened Fear Of School Shootings, It's Not A Growing Epidemic," NPR, March 15, 2018, https://www.npr.org/2018/03/15/593831564/the-disconnect-between-perceived-danger-in-u-s-schools-and-reality

[338] Ibid.

[339] Ibid.

[340] Ibid.

[341] Ibid.

[342] "School shootings are not the new normal, despite statistics that stretch the truth," *USA Today*, February 19, 2018, https://www.usatoday.com/story/opinion/2018/02/19/parkla nd-school-shootings-not-new-normal-despite-statistics-stretching-truth-fox-column/349380002/

[343] "There Is No 'Epidemic of Mass School Shootings," *New York Magazine*, March 1, 2018, http://nymag.com/daily/intelligencer/2018/03/there-is-no-epidemic-of-mass-school-shootings.html

[344] Ibid.

[345] "Ronald Reagan: Over '20,000 Gun Control Laws' Yet Hinckley Had a Gun," *Breitbart*, May 31, 2016, http://www.breitbart.com/big-government/2016/05/31/ronald-reagan-20000-gun-control-laws-yet-hinckley-got-gun/

[346] Fact Sheet - Federal Firearms and Explosives Licenses by Types, Bureau of Alcohol, Tobacco, Firearms and Explosives, May 2018, https://www.atf.gov/resource-center/fact-sheet/fact-sheet-federal-firearms-and-explosives-licenses-types

[347] "Hunting and Hearing Loss," Starkey Hearing Technologies, August 31, 2015, https://www.starkey.com/blog/2015/08/hunting-and-hearing-loss

[348] "5 Steps to Purchase a Silencer," Silencer Co., https://silencerco.com/blog/2016/03/10/5-simple-steps-to-purchase-a-silencer/

[349] "Clinton signed the Brady Handgun Violence Prevention Act, Nov 30, 1993," *Politico*, November 30, 2012, https://www.politico.com/story/2012/11/this-day-in-politics-084414

[350] U.S. Department of Justice, Firearms Transaction Record, https://www.atf.gov/firearms/docs/4473-part-1-firearms-

transaction-record-over-counter-atf-form-53009/download;
"How gun background checks work," CNN, February 15,
2018, https://www.cnn.com/2018/02/15/us/gun-
background-checks-florida-school-shooting/index.html

351 Firearm Owners Protection Act, 18 USC 926; "Background
checks on gun sales: How do they work?" CNN, April 10,
2013,
https://www.cnn.com/2013/04/10/politics/background-
checks-explainer/index.html

352 "Massive noncompliance with SAFE Act," *Hudson Valley One*,
July 7, 2016,
https://hudsonvalleyone.com/2016/07/07/massive-
noncompliance-with-safe-act/

353 "State Can't Let Gun Scofflaws Off Hook," *Hartford Courant*,
February 14, 2014, http://articles.courant.com/2014-02-
14/news/hc-ed-gun-registration-20140214_1_new-law-gun-
registration-military-style-assault-weapons

354 Stephen P. Halbrook, "How the Nazis Used Gun Control,"
National Review, December 2, 2013
https://www.nationalreview.com/2013/12/how-nazis-used-
gun-control-stephen-p-halbrook/

355 "Firearms Registration: New York City's Lesson," January 27, 2000,
https://www.nraila.org/articles/20000127/firearms-registration-
new-york-city-s

356 March for our Lives, Mission Statement,
https://marchforourlives.com/mission-statement/

357 "Crude Suicide Rate by Country 2018" World Population
Review, www.worldpopulationreview.com/countries/suicide-
rate-by-country/

358 Ibid.

359 Ibid.

360 Kids Count Data Center, Total population by child and adult
populations, https://datacenter.kidscount.org/data/tables/99-
total-population-by-child-and-

adult#detailed/1/any/false/870,573,869,36,868,867,133,38,3 5,18/39,40,41/416,417

361 Centers for Disease Control, National Vital Statistics System, February 19, 2017, https://webappa.cdc.gov/sasweb/ncipc/dataRestriction_inj.ht ml; "Accidental gun deaths hit record low, even amid recent boom in firearms sales" Fox News, March 30, 2017, http://www.foxnews.com/politics/2017/03/30/as-gun-sales-rise-accidental-gun-deaths-drop-to-record-levels-report-says.html

362 Centers for Disease Control, National Vital Statistics System, February 19, 2017, https://webappa.cdc.gov/sasweb/ncipc/dataRestriction_inj.ht ml.

363 Ibid.

364 Ibid.

365 Ibid.

366 Ibid.

367 Ibid.

368 *The Bias Against Guns: Why Almost Everything You've Heard About Guns is Wrong*, John R. Lott, Jr., Regnery Publishing, 2003, p. 83-84, https://books.google.com/books?id=LeM6ljmnfQEC&pg=P A84&lpg=PA84&dq=The+Bias+Against+Guns+children+un der+five+drowned+in+five-gallon+plastic+water+buckets&source=bl&ots=N8qWs4HIZ m&sig=2xd9OgRotpVfVmzeNlxRE6dRgmU&hl=en&sa=X &ved=0ahUKEwi5qfyK8pfbAhWMjlkKHeMPBFwQ6AEI LjAB#v=onepage&q=The%20Bias%20Against%20Guns%20 children%20under%20five%20drowned%20in%20five-gallon%20plastic%20water%20buckets&f=false

369 Everytown for Gun Safety, https://everytownresearch.org/gun-violence-by-the-numbers/#KidsTeens

370 Ibid.; Brady Campaign to Prevent Gun Violence, http://www.bradycampaign.org/key-gun-violence-statistics;

371 Brady Campaign to Prevent Gun Violence,
http://www.bradycampaign.org/key-gun-violence-statistics;
"Do seven children per day die from guns?" *Politifact
California,* December 27, 2016,
http://www.politifact.com/california/statements/2016/dec/27
/jackie-speier/examining-claim-7-children-day-die-gun-
violence/

372 Everytown for Gun Safety, https://everytownresearch.org/gun-
violence-by-the-numbers/#KidsTeens

373 "From arson to drug robberies, teens are killing and being killed
in Indianapolis," *The Indianapolis Star,* November 9, 2017,
https://www.indystar.com/story/news/crime/2017/11/09/tee
n-violence-indianapolis-crime-news-shooting-recent-
murders-impd/840919001/; Key Facts About Youth
Violence, Official Site of the Los Angeles Police Department
http://www.lapdonline.org/search_results/content_basic_vie
w/23514; "See Chicago's Deadly Year in 3 Charts," *TIME,*
January 17, 2017, http://time.com/4635049/chicago-murder-
rate-homicides/

374 Teen Violence Statistics,
http://www.teenviolencestatistics.com/content/gang-
violence.html

375 Morgan Bennett, "Internet Pornography & the First
Amendment," The Witherspoon Institute, Public Discourse,
October 10, 2013,
http://www.thepublicdiscourse.com/2013/10/10998/

376 Daniel Schultz, Lectric Law Library, The Second Amendment:
The Framers' Intentions,
https://www.lectlaw.com/files/gun01.htm

377 Matt MacBradaigh, "Gun Control Myth: The Second
Amendment Makes Clear Guns Aren't Just For the
Military," *Mic,* January 28, 2013,
https://mic.com/articles/24210/gun-control-myth-the-
second-amendment-makes-clear-guns-aren-t-just-for-the-
military#.bdrjaYrqW

378 *District of Columbia v. Heller,* 554 U.S. 570 (2008); "Of Course
the Second Amendment Protects an Individual Right to

Keep and Bear Arms," *National Review*, April 13, 2016,
https://www.nationalreview.com/2016/04/second-
amendment-protects-individual-right-keep-bear-arms/

[379] "Whether the Second Amendment Secures an Individual
Right," Department of Justice, Memorandum Opinion for
the Attorney General, August 24, 2004,
https://www.justice.gov/file/18831/download

[380] "John Paul Stevens: Repeal the Second Amendment," *The New
York Times*, March 27, 2018,
https://www.nytimes.com/2018/03/27/opinion/john-paul-
stevens-repeal-second-amendment.html

[381] "How They Got Their Guns," *The New York Times*, February
16, 2018,
https://www.nytimes.com/interactive/2015/10/03/us/how-
mass-shooters-got-their-guns.html

[382] "Parkland student Kyle Kashuv claims he was interrogated by
deputy, school security after shooting AR-15 at gun range,"
Sun Sentinal, April 25, 2018, http://www.sun-
sentinel.com/local/broward/parkland/florida-school-
shooting/fl-reg-parkland-student-draws-fire-for-shooting-
ar15-at-gun-range-20180425-story.html

[383] "WHY THE 2ND AMENDMENT APPLIES ONLY TO
YOUR MUSKETS AND DUELING PISTOLS," *Ozy*,
October 4, 2016, https://www.ozy.com/immodest-
proposal/why-the-2nd-amendment-applies-only-to-your-
muskets-and-dueling-pistols/72045

[384] "Before Gatling – Who Was The First To Invent A Rapid-Fire
Gun?" *Military History Now*, January 27, 2014,
https://militaryhistorynow.com/2014/01/27/before-gatling-
who-was-the-first-to-invent-the-rapid-fire-gun/; "Thomas
Jefferson's 'Assault Rifle' – The Girardoni Air Rifle," *The
Federalist Papers*, June 11, 2014,
https://thefederalistpapers.org/founders/jefferson/thomas-
jeffersons-assault-rifle-the-girardoni-air-rifle

[385] "Supreme Court orders SJC to reconsider stun gun ruling," *The
Boston Globe*, March 21, 2016,
https://www.bostonglobe.com/metro/2016/03/21/supreme-

court-orders-mass-high-court-reconsider-stun-gun-
ruling/RtA9pHtavuYhzXw9KPotCM/story.html

386 Ibid.

387 *Caetano v. Massachusetts*, 554 U.S. 570 (2008).
https://www.law.cornell.edu/supremecourt/text/14-10078

388 Ibid.

389 Ibid.

390 *District of Columbia v. Heller*, 554 U.S. 570 (2008).
https://supreme.justia.com/cases/federal/us/554/570/

391 Darrin Weaver, "Viet Cong Weaponry: 14 Small Arms From
the Vietnam War," *Tactical Life*, October 22, 2015,
https://www.tactical-life.com/firearms/viet-cong-weaponry-
14-vietnam-war/

392 H. R. Trevor-Roper, ed., *Hitler's Table Talk, 1941–1944* (New
York: Enigma Books, 2000–2008), 321.

393 "Hitler vs. Stalin: Who Killed More?" *The New York Review of
Books*, March 10, 2011,
http://www.nybooks.com/articles/2011/03/10/hitler-vs-
stalin-who-killed-more/

394 *Quotations from Chairman Mao* (Peking: Foreign Languages
Press, 1972), 61, 102.

395 "Mao's Great Leap Forward 'killed 45 million in four years',"
Independent, September 17, 2010,
http://www.nybooks.com/articles/2011/03/10/hitler-vs-
stalin-who-killed-more/

396 Benito Mussolini, The First Six Months in Office, Speech in
the Chamber, June 8, 1923
http://bibliotecafascista.blogspot.com/2012/03/speech-in-
chamber-june-8-1923.html

397 Joseph Stalin, THE FIFTEENTH CONGRESS OF THE
C.P.S.U.(B.), December 2-19, 1927,
http://marx2mao.com/Stalin/FC27.html#s5iii

398 "Hitler vs. Stalin: Who Killed More?" *The New York Review of Books*, March 10, 2011, http://www.nybooks.com/articles/2011/03/10/hitler-vs-stalin-who-killed-more/

399 Aleksandr Solzhenitsyn, *The Gulag Archipelago 1918-1956*, https://www.goodreads.com/quotes/34738-and-how-we-burned-in-the-camps-later-thinking-what

400 *Silveira v. Lockyer*, 328 F.3d 567 (9th Cir. 2003), https://law.justia.com/cases/federal/appellate-courts/F3/328/567/500155/

401 Ibid.

402 Stephen P. Halbrook "How the Nazis Used Gun Control," *National Review*, December 2, 2013, https://www.nationalreview.com/2013/12/how-nazis-used-gun-control-stephen-p-halbrook/

403 Ibid.

404 Ibid.

405 Ibid.

406 Ibid.

407 Ian Janssen, Steven B. Heymsfield, ZiMian Wang, and Robert Ross, "Skeletal muscle mass and distribution in 468 men and women aged 18–88 yr," *Journal of Applied Physiology*, July 1, 2000, https://www.physiology.org/doi/abs/10.1152/jappl.2000.89.1.81

408 "Mike Tyson explains one of his most famous quotes," *Sun Sentinal*, November 9, 2012, http://articles.sun-sentinel.com/2012-11-09/sports/sfl-mike-tyson-explains-one-of-his-most-famous-quotes-20121109_1_mike-tyson-undisputed-truth-famous-quotes

409 U.S. Fire Administration, Fire Statistics 2015, https://www.usfa.fema.gov/data/statistics/#tab-1; FBI, 2016 Crime Statistics Released,

https://www.fbi.gov/news/stories/2016-crime-statistics-released

[410] Kay Coles James, "Let's get serious about school safety," Heritage Foundation, March 2018, https://www.heritage.org/school-safety

[411] National Institute of Justice, U.S. Department of Justice, June 17, 2014, https://www.nij.gov/topics/corrections/recidivism/Pages/welcome.aspx

About the Author

Mark W. Smith is *The New York Times* bestselling author of *The Official Handbook of the Vast Right-Wing Conspiracy: The Arguments You Need to Defeat the Loony Left*. He is a Presidential Scholar and Senior Fellow in Law and Public Policy at The King's College in New York City as well as a former professor of law. Smith is a practicing trial attorney who is admitted to the U.S. Supreme Court Bar and serves as the vice president of the New York City chapter of the Federalist Society, the nation's most prominent conservative legal organization. Smith, a graduate of the New York University School of Law, regularly appears in the national media as a political and legal commentator. His book *Disrobed: The New Battle Plan to Break the Left's Stranglehold on the Courts* lays out an aggressive approach to thwart the liberal assault on America. He lives in New York City with his 12-pound gun dog, Hugo.